P9-AQW-610

Play Ball

100 Baseball Practice Games

Tom O'Connell

Human Kinetics

Library of Congress Cataloging-in-Publication Data

O'Connell, Tom.
  Play ball : 100 baseball practice games / Tom O'Connell.
    p. cm.
  ISBN-13: 978-0-7360-8157-3 (soft cover)
  ISBN-10: 0-7360-8157-7 (soft cover)
  1. Baseball for children--Training. 2. Baseball for children--Coaching. I. Title.
  GV880.4.O46 2010
  796.357'62--dc22

                                      2009035768

ISBN-10: 0-7360-8157-7 (print)
ISBN-13: 978-0-7360-8157-3 (print)

Copyright © 2010 by Human Kinetics, Inc.

All rights reserved. Except for use in a review, the reproduction or utilization of this work in any form or by any electronic, mechanical, or other means, now known or hereafter invented, including xerography, photocopying, and recording, and in any information storage and retrieval system, is forbidden without the written permission of the publisher.

Acquisitions Editor: Justin Klug; **Developmental Editor:** Anne Hall; **Assistant Editor:** Cory Weber; **Copyeditor:** Bob Replinger; **Graphic Designer:** Joe Buck; **Graphic Artist:** Tara Welsch; **Cover Designer:** Keith Blomberg; **Photographer (cover):** Human Kinetics; **Art Manager:** Kelly Hendren; **Associate Art Manager:** Alan L. Wilborn; **Printer:** Sheridan Books

Human Kinetics books are available at special discounts for bulk purchase. Special editions or book excerpts can also be created to specification. For details, contact the Special Sales Manager at Human Kinetics.

Printed in the United States of America   10 9 8 7 6 5 4 3 2 1

The paper in this book is certified under a sustainable forestry program.

Human Kinetics
Web site: www.HumanKinetics.com

United States: Human Kinetics
P.O. Box 5076
Champaign, IL 61825-5076
800-747-4457
e-mail: humank@hkusa.com

Canada: Human Kinetics
475 Devonshire Road Unit 100
Windsor, ON N8Y 2L5
800-465-7301 (in Canada only)
e-mail: info@hkcanada.com

Europe: Human Kinetics
107 Bradford Road
Stanningley
Leeds LS28 6AT, United Kingdom
+44 (0) 113 255 5665
e-mail: hk@hkeurope.com

Australia: Human Kinetics
57A Price Avenue
Lower Mitcham, South Australia 5062
08 8372 0999
e-mail: info@hkaustralia.com

New Zealand: Human Kinetics
P.O. Box 80
Torrens Park, South Australia 5062
0800 222 062
e-mail: info@hknewzealand.com

E4753

Contents

Game Finder   iv

Key   ix

Introduction   x

1 Throwing Games **1**

2 Infield Games . . . . **.29**

3 Outfield Games . . . . **.67**

4 Pitching Games . . . . **.89**

5 Catching Games **111**

6 Hitting Games **133**

7 Situational Games **167**

8 Team Games **193**

9 Practice Planning **215**

About the Author   226

Game Finder

#	Game	Defensive Skills				Offensive Skills			Strategy	Age	Skill Level	Page
		Throwing	Receiving	Pitching	Footwork	Bunting	Hitting	Baserunning				
Chapter 1 Throwing Games												
1.1	Four Corners	✓	✓							All	All	2
1.2	Hit the Target Squarely	✓	✓							All		4
1.3	Yoga Toss	✓	✓							All	All, especially beginners	6
1.4	One-Knee Throwing	✓	✓							All	All	8
1.5	Whoosh	✓								All	All, especially beginners	10
1.6	Touch 'Em All	✓					✓	✓	D	8 and older		12
1.7	Doubles	✓					✓	✓	D	8 and older		14
1.8	Progressive Long Toss	✓	✓							All		16
1.9	Four Corners Against the Clock	✓	✓							12 and older		18
1.10	Globetrotter	✓	✓							12 and older		20
1.11	Stars	✓	✓						D	12 and older		22
1.12	Soft Hands	✓	✓							High school and older		24
1.13	Cutoff and Relay Throw Race	✓	✓						D	12 and older		26

Strategy: D = Defense; O = Offense; B = Both offense and defense

Skill Level: ![basic] = Basic; ![basic-intermediate] = Basic to Intermediate; ![intermediate] = Intermediate; ![intermediate-advanced] = Intermediate to Advanced; ![advanced] = Advanced

#	Game	Defensive Skills				Offensive Skills			Strategy	Age	Skill Level	Page
		Throwing	Receiving	Pitching	Footwork	Bunting	Hitting	Baserunning				
Chapter 2 Infield Games												
2.1	Backhand Force	✓			✓				D	12 and older	Advanced (5)	30
2.2	Balls in the Dirt		✓		✓					High school and older	Intermediate to Advanced (4)	32
2.3	Crossover		✓		✓					All	All	34
2.4	Double-Play Rotation	✓	✓		✓				D	12 and older	Intermediate to Advanced (4)	36
2.5	Enhanced Crossover	✓	✓		✓					10 and older	All	38
2.6	Follow the Bouncing Ball		✓		✓					All	Basic (1)	40
2.7	Get 50!	✓	✓		✓					10 and older	Basic (1)	42
2.8	Get There!		✓		✓					All	All	44
2.9	The Hot Box		✓		✓					All	All	46
2.10	Goalie		✓		✓					All	Basic to Intermediate (2)	48
2.11	Hold and Go	✓	✓		✓				D	12 and older	Intermediate to Advanced (4)	50
2.12	Hot-Corner Reaction		✓		✓					High school and older	Intermediate to Advanced (4)	52
2.13	Hot Shots		✓		✓				D	12 and older	Intermediate to Advanced (4)	54
2.14	Mass Fungo		✓		✓					12 and older	Basic to Intermediate (2)	56
2.15	PFP (With a Twist)	✓	✓		✓				D	High school and older	Intermediate to Advanced (4)	58
2.16	Slow-Roller Throwing	✓								High school and older	Intermediate to Advanced (4)	60
2.17	Spin and Fire	✓			✓				D	12 and older	Advanced (5)	62
2.18	Z Ball Reaction		✓		✓					High school and older	Intermediate to Advanced (4)	64

Strategy: D = Defense; O = Offense; B = Both offense and defense

Skill Level: 🏐 = Basic; 🏐🏐 = Basic to Intermediate; 🏐🏐🏐 = Intermediate; 🏐🏐🏐🏐 = Intermediate to Advanced; 🏐🏐🏐🏐🏐 = Advanced

#	Game	Defensive Skills				Offensive Skills			Strategy	Age	Skill Level	Page
		Throwing	Receiving	Pitching	Footwork	Bunting	Hitting	Baserunning				
Chapter 3 Outfield Games												
3.1	Two-Line Communication		✓						D	All	All	68
3.2	Five Alive		✓		✓					12 and older	⚾⚾⚾	70
3.3	Harvey's Wallbanger	✓	✓		✓				D	12 and older	⚾⚾⚾	72
3.4	Hustle!		✓		✓					10 and older	⚾⚾	74
3.5	Do or Die	✓	✓		✓					12 and older	⚾⚾⚾⚾	76
3.6	Cut 'Em Down	✓	✓		✓				D	12 and older	⚾⚾⚾⚾	78
3.7	Line Drive		✓		✓					12 and older	⚾⚾⚾⚾	80
3.8	Fence		✓		✓				D	12 and older	⚾⚾⚾⚾	82
3.9	Turn and Burn		✓		✓					12 and older	⚾⚾⚾⚾	84
3.10	Tweeners		✓		✓				D	12 and older	⚾⚾⚾⚾	86
Chapter 4 Pitching Games												
4.1	Diamond and One	✓	✓	✓	✓				D	12 and older	⚾⚾⚾⚾	90
4.2	In the Box			✓					D	12 and older	⚾⚾⚾⚾	92
4.3	Location, Location, Location			✓					D	12 and older	⚾⚾⚾⚾	94
4.4	Pickoff Rotation	✓	✓		✓				B	12 and older	⚾⚾⚾⚾	96
4.5	Pitcher's Duel			✓					D	High school and older	⚾⚾⚾⚾	98
4.6	Smash Ball		✓	✓					D	12 and older	⚾⚾⚾⚾	100
4.7	Dueling Pitchers (U-R-O-U-T)			✓					D	12 and older	⚾⚾⚾⚾	102
4.8	Pitching by Script			✓					D	12 and older	⚾⚾⚾⚾⚾	104
4.9	Pick at Two	✓	✓	✓	✓				B	12 and older	⚾⚾⚾⚾⚾	106
4.10	In and Out, Up and Down			✓					D	High school and older	⚾⚾⚾⚾⚾	108

Strategy: D = Defense; O = Offense; B = Both offense and defense

Skill Level: ⚾ = Basic; ⚾⚾ = Basic to Intermediate; ⚾⚾⚾ = Intermediate; ⚾⚾⚾⚾ = Intermediate to Advanced; ⚾⚾⚾⚾⚾ = Advanced

#	Game	Defensive Skills				Offensive Skills			Strategy	Age	Skill Level	Page
		Throwing	Receiving	Pitching	Footwork	Bunting	Hitting	Baserunning				
Chapter 5 Catching Games												
5.1	Catcher Challenge		✓		✓					12 and older	⚾⚾	112
5.2	Fielding Bunts	✓	✓		✓				D	10 and older	⚾⚾	114
5.3	Guard the Castle		✓		✓					10 and older	⚾⚾	116
5.4	Sway and Frame		✓							10 and older	⚾⚾	118
5.5	Egg Drop		✓		✓				D	12 and older	⚾⚾⚾⚾	120
5.6	Tag and Score		✓		✓			✓	B	12 and older	⚾⚾⚾⚾	122
5.7	Transfer and Let It Fly	✓	✓							12 and older	⚾⚾⚾⚾	124
5.8	Wild Pitch	✓	✓		✓			✓	B	12 and older	⚾⚾⚾⚾	126
5.9	Pick 'Em	✓	✓		✓				D	12 and older	⚾⚾⚾⚾⚾	128
5.10	Rapid Fire		✓							12 and older	⚾⚾⚾⚾	130
Chapter 6 Hitting Games												
6.1	Target Hitting						✓			10 and older	All	134
6.2	Over the Line						✓		O	8 and older	⚾⚾	136
6.3	Flip It						✓			10 and older	All	138
6.4	Three-Man Bunting				✓	✓			O	12 and older	⚾⚾	140
6.5	Wastebasket Bunting					✓			O	10 and older	All	142
6.6	Four-Corner Bunting	✓	✓			✓		✓	O	12 and older	⚾⚾⚾⚾	144
6.7	Hit the Target						✓		O	12 and older	⚾⚾⚾⚾	146
6.8	Pepper		✓		✓		✓			12 and older	⚾⚾⚾⚾	148
6.9	Read the Pitch						✓		O	12 and older	⚾⚾⚾⚾	150
6.10	Short Toss				✓		✓		O	12 and older	⚾⚾⚾⚾	152
6.11	Right Side		✓		✓		✓		O	12 and older	⚾⚾⚾⚾	154

Strategy: D = Defense; O = Offense; B = Both offense and defense

Skill Level: ⚾ = Basic; ⚾⚾ = Basic to Intermediate; ⚾⚾⚾ = Intermediate; ⚾⚾⚾⚾ = Intermediate to Advanced; ⚾⚾⚾⚾⚾ = Advanced

#	Game	Throwing	Receiving	Pitching	Footwork	Bunting	Hitting	Baserunning	Strategy	Age	Skill Level	Page
		Defensive Skills				Offensive Skills						
	**Chapter 6 Hitting Games (continued)**											
6.12	Top Hand, Bottom Hand						✓			12 and older	(4 balls)	156
6.13	Triangle Hitting	✓			✓		✓		O	12 and older	(4 balls)	158
6.14	Walk-Through						✓			12 and older	(4 balls)	160
6.15	Timing Sticks						✓			12 and older	(5 balls)	162
6.16	Speed Stik						✓			12 and older	(5 balls)	164
6.17	Take or Hit			✓			✓		O	12 and older	(4 balls)	166
	**Chapter 7 Situational Games**											
7.1	Pickle	✓	✓		✓			✓	B	10 and older	(2 balls)	168
7.2	0-2 Breaking Ball		✓	✓				✓	B	12 and older	(4 balls)	170
7.3	Advancing From Second	✓	✓	✓	✓			✓	B	12 and older	(4 balls)	172
7.4	Cat and Mouse	✓	✓	✓				✓	B	12 and older	(4 balls)	174
7.5	Contact	✓			✓			✓	B	12 and older	(4 balls)	176
7.6	In the Hole			✓			✓		B	12 and older	(4 balls)	178
7.7	Long Tee				✓		✓		O	12 and older	(4 balls)	180
7.8	Overthrow							✓	O	12 and older	(4 balls)	182
7.9	Bobble and Go!							✓	O	12 and older	(4 balls)	184
7.10	Read and Run	✓	✓		✓			✓	O	12 and older	(4 balls)	186
7.11	Take Three	✓						✓	B	12 and older	(4 balls)	188
7.12	Long Pepper				✓		✓		O	12 and older	(5 balls)	190

Strategy: D = Defense; O = Offense; B = Both offense and defense

Skill Level: (1 ball) = Basic; (2 balls) = Basic to Intermediate; (3 balls) = Intermediate; (4 balls) = Intermediate to Advanced; (5 balls) = Advanced

#	Game	Defensive Skills				Offensive Skills			Strategy	Age	Skill Level	Page
		Throwing	Receiving	Pitching	Footwork	Bunting	Hitting	Baserunning				
	Chapter 8 Team Games											
8.1	Keystone Cops	✓	✓		✓		✓		B	All	All	194
8.2	Move Up	✓	✓		✓		✓	✓	B	10 and older	All	196
8.3	Situations	✓	✓		✓			✓	B	10 and older	All	198
8.4	21 Outs	✓	✓	✓	✓		✓	✓	B	12 and older	⚾⚾⚾⚾	200
8.5	Bingo, Bango, Bongo	✓	✓		✓	✓	✓	✓	O	12 and older	⚾⚾⚾⚾	202
8.6	Bunt Game	✓	✓		✓	✓		✓	B	12 and older	⚾⚾⚾⚾	204
8.7	Combat Scrimmage	✓	✓	✓	✓	✓	✓	✓	B	12 and older	⚾⚾⚾⚾	206
8.8	Hit-and-Run	✓	✓		✓		✓	✓	B	12 and older	⚾⚾⚾⚾	208
8.9	Relay, Relay, Relay	✓			✓			✓	B	12 and older	⚾⚾⚾⚾	210
8.10	Double-Steal Challenge	✓	✓	✓	✓			✓	B	12 and older	⚾⚾⚾⚾⚾	212

Strategy: D = Defense; O = Offense; B = Both offense and defense

Skill Level: ⚾ = Basic; ⚾⚾ = Basic to Intermediate; ⚾⚾⚾ = Intermediate; ⚾⚾⚾⚾ = Intermediate to Advanced; ⚾⚾⚾⚾⚾ = Advanced

Key

Player	Batter	Cone	- - - → Throw
Coach	Runner	Pitching machine	⟶ Player movement
Fielder	Bucket	∿⟶ Ground ball	∿⟶ Running
		⋯⟶ Fly ball	Tee

Introduction

Over the years I've gone to many clinics and listened to some outstanding speakers give excellent talks about great drills. And at those same clinics, I've had many conversations with my coaching friends from all over the country about using those drills and the best way to teach the game. Through the years of clinics and hot-stove discussions, one thought kept irritating me. Why is it that at practice we work on drill after drill after drill, our players master the drills and look better and better, but they keep making the same mistakes in games? Maybe, I thought, they are just getting better at doing drills. The science of coaching has improved 10-fold in the last 40 years, but fewer of our players seem capable of playing the game at a high level. The lapses of concentration, the mistakes in judgment, and the failure to execute often plague our teams and players. Was it my fault? Was I working the players hard enough or concentrating on the right skills in practice? Finally, out of frustration, after the umpteenth time one of my players failed to execute a bunt in a crucial game situation, I took a long, hard look at the way that I was teaching bunting.

Every year, at least once a week, we worked on bunting in practice—dry drills, partner drills, bunting before batting practice, bunting after batting practice, bunting in hallways, bunting in the gym. Yet even after all that practice there were too many times when I gave the bunt sign in a game and a player failed to execute. He would hit the ball hard right back to the pitcher or miss it completely or, even worse, pop it up. I chalked it up to a lack of focus, a lack of skill, or a lack of belief in the importance of bunting—the same explanations that my coaching peers offered when we met at clinics. Too many video games, we said. Too many distractions. Too little effort.

Our kids just didn't have baseball sense, as I called it—what some would call baseball IQ. Besides having crucial letdowns in key situations, players seemed to miss the little nuances of the game—the ability to anticipate that something will happen before it does. I knew that the players I had were smart. I keep track of their academic progress all the time. It wasn't that they couldn't think; it was that they weren't always aware.

And then I had an epiphany. Could it be that the root cause of the problem might lie in the word *teaching*? Nothing was wrong with the way my assistant coaches and I were teaching bunting. Nothing was wrong with the way we taught fielding. The problem was that we were *teaching* it when the emphasis should have been on the players' *learning* it. The burden was on the wrong half of the equation. As coaches, we should have learned our lesson. Forty years ago, as teachers, we discovered that the lecture method, another term for direct instruction, wasn't the best way to reach young learners. Ever since, the classroom has been a place where good teachers avoid giving lectures; instead, they facilitate learning.

Forty years ago a revolution also took place in baseball instruction. When I was in high school, teams spent most practice time running, taking batting practice, taking infield and outfield, and then running some more. Then in the 1960s and 1970s a new era of instruction began. Articles and books flooded the market touting drills that could teach skills. And they were fine books written by excellent coaches—Dick Siebert, Danny Litwhiler, and Bob Shaw, to name a few. The era of the scientific approach to baseball began. But somewhere in that transition, from the good ol' days of practice to the science of baseball, something got lost—baseball IQ, or the ability of players to sense and unconsciously react to changes in the game around them.

So in the classroom as we were getting away from the direct approach, on the athletic field we never gave it up. I believe that it is time for coaches to start imitating the methods that work in the classroom! Just as mastering multiplication tables doesn't mean students have learned math, mastering the mechanical skills of baseball, although important, doesn't mean that players have learned the game. They need to learn not only how to play the game technically but also how to connect the dots tactically. Most baseball texts overlook these tactical aspects. Coaches even omit them from practice regularly because they become focused on technical skills. They develop tunnel vision and lose sight of the strategies that players need to understand. Besides, teaching tactics is harder and takes much more effort than teaching technique.

After the light bulb went on above my head, I reassessed the way that I ran practices and what my own players were doing. For years, I had been using a game I called Situations (chapter 8). I used it at the end of practice as a challenge to my defense. It was gamelike, seemed to help my players learn, and gave me a chance to see how they ran the bases and reacted to batted balls. I have always thought that it was an effective use of practice time. The players responded to it well—in fact, they had fun playing it. Hmmm? I looked at other drills that we used in practice and thought of ways to make them more like my Situations game—challenging and at game speed. Somewhere around the same time I heard about a technique being used in gym classes called TGfU (Teaching Games for Understanding) based on the work of pioneering British professors David Bunker and Rod Thorpe. That work in turn led me to the games approach, articulated first by Australian pole vault coach Alan Launder in his seminal book *Play Practice: The Games Approach to Teaching and Coaching Sports* and enhanced more recently by Rainer Martens in *Successful Coaching*. Bam! Suddenly, a whole philosophy of practice approach landed in my lap and started to make sense. There was another way of doing things—a way that was more gamelike. That's why Situations worked. I became convinced that the best way to make my players into better thinkers was to let them play more games. If, as my coaching buddies and I thought, kids don't play the game enough, why not let them play the game more in practice? That approach might help them become better thinkers, become players with game sense. This newer paradigm of play practice, the games approach, is discussed by coaches Launder and Martens in their own books. For a detailed and thorough exposition of these methods, I urge readers to consult those two texts.

Traditional Approach

Most of us follow a model of practice that has produced great benefits for us over the years. The paradigm of the traditional method is tried and true. Practice starts with a little stretching and a little running. A throwing warm-up follows. Then we pick a skill that we need to work on. Maybe in the last game, the team didn't handle relays and cutoffs well, so in practice we start with a relay drill, focusing on hitting the cutoff, throwing with good technique, getting the feet in position to throw before receiving the ball, and so on. From there, perhaps we move into other drills that cover skills that need retooling—the double play, bunting, pickoffs at second, and so forth. We follow those up with batting practice. We keep everyone busy with stations leading up to hitting on the field. They take 10 cuts, or 15 cuts. During batting practice, we give our pitchers work by having them throw to hitters or letting them throw on the side. After batting practice, we have the daily scrimmage, or we finish up with infield and outfield practice. We might throw in some physical training at the end—running bases, doing sprints—and then everyone grabs a rake. We police the field and then send everyone off to the showers. Some days we eliminate the scrimmage and do more drill work, hoping to get the kinks out of the bad plays that occurred during our last game, but practice is largely the same every day.

This model has worked for many teams. It is organized and moves from point to point well, but it does have shortcomings. For one it overemphasizes mechanical skills. Our players might become better at fielding techniques or double-play pivots or playing the ball off the wall, but at what expense? The traditional approach also puts too much stress on direct instruction. The coach tells players what to do and how to do it. It also relies heavily on the use of drills—usually out of context of the game. Often, the result is that players learn how to do drills well but can't execute the same skill with proficiency in the game. Every coach has seen players jump into the batting cage in practice and tear the cover off the ball on the tees or against the pitching machine but then have trouble making good contact once the game begins. This type of hitter has learned the art of performing well in drills but has not learned how to transfer those technical skills to the tactical situations that they face when at bat during a game. Some people call this choking, but a more accurate description would be a failure to adapt. The same sort of thing happens to the player who can field every ground ball flawlessly in practice but bobbles easy grounders in a game or lets them go through his legs. These examples show that sometimes players haven't been able to translate the work in the cage or during infield drills into game situations. This transfer of learning is a key in education today and should be a key in coaching.

Drills also stand the risk of being boring, especially when repeated without change from one practice to the next. I've seen players going through the motions with a drill even on the first day of practice because, as they say, "We've done this before."

Drills should have a prominent place in practice, but they should not be the focus. Drills work well at times, especially when teaching a skill for the first time or when trying to lower the risk of injury. Teaching players how to slide or how to drag bunt might fall into this category. The best way to teach these skills would be to (1) explain the skill, (2) model it, and (3) create a drill for the players to work on the skill, all along providing good feedback.

Games Approach

But practice that focuses on drills, live hitting, and scrimmaging does not increase players' baseball sense. The alternative approach, the games approach, helps your players become smarter and puts the coach squarely in the role of facilitator, not commander in chief. This method allows players to learn the game through enjoyable learning activities featuring gamelike practices that create realistic situations through which they can develop baseball sense.

This book incorporates the three major components in the games approach into the practice games. The first of these elements is shaping—taking a drill and tweaking it a little so that it fits the purposes of the skill that you want the players to learn. This can be done by changing the rules, changing the number of players involved, changing the size of the playing field, modifying the objective of the game and scoring, or modifying the equipment used. Knowing how the tactic fits into the team's game or season plan also helps players buy into the tactic. Coaches can assist their athletes with this by providing them with clear objectives and explaining how learning these objectives elevates their capability to play and helps their team win games. When play is shaped—say, for example, by reducing the number of players—the weaker players are put into positions where they will have more opportunities to play active roles. In short, shaping means redesigning the game.

The second element of the games approach is focusing play. This means that a coach can stop the game at any time to explain a point or correct mistakes in judgment. Using the Bunt Game (chapter 8) as an example, if a fielder in a sacrifice situation bunts the ball back hard to the pitcher, enabling the pitcher to make a play on a lead runner, then the coach can stop the game and point out to the bunter why the bunt was unsuccessful. The player, we hope, will not do the same thing the next time. If a fielder tries to make a play that might be beyond his physical limitations or not appropriate for that moment in the game, the coach can use a freeze replay to put the play into perspective. Freeze replays are crucial to the concept of the games approach. Simply put, they capitalize on teachable moments, the mantra of the classroom, and give the coach an opportunity to put the players and the ball back into the positions where they were when the tactical error occurred and have the players note the situation. Then by questioning players about why they were doing what they were, the coach can let the players come to the realization themselves about why their actions were incorrect. This method gives players the responsibility for solving the dilemma of the situation, which in turn helps them build their baseball IQ.

The final element of the games approach is enhancing play. This goal can be accomplished by challenging players further than they will be challenged in games. Limiting the area into which they can hit or handicapping drills helps keep the games competitive. Games like Long Tee in chapter 7 or Triangle Hitting in chapter 6 effectively limit where a player can hit. Using the Bunt Game as an example again, placing cones on the field to delineate a hitting area further limits and focuses players on their bunting skills. Not allowing fielders to charge, even when they know that a bunt is coming, challenges the defense even more. All the games in this book test players' mettle by having them compete against their partners, part of the team, or the whole team. These challenges enhance practice and build players' baseball IQ.

How can the games approach work for you and your practices? Most of the games in this book are derived from drills that I've used for years. But I've tried to give all of them an element of competition that they were lacking before. Take some of the drills in this book or drills that you like to use and make them more competitive. Shape them so that they accomplish more than just having players work on technique. Use freeze replays often, especially in situation games or scrimmages and let your players come up with the solutions. I know that many of us learned the game under the philosophy that baseball is not a democracy. The my-way-or-the-highway approach hinders our players from exploring, learning, and developing baseball sense. They have to learn for themselves what works and what doesn't. And they have to learn in a caring, safe environment where they have plenty of chance to succeed. A good coach, like a good teacher, can use the questioning method and have players come up with the right answers. We just have to ask the right questions.

Games such as those in this book teach players to play the game, not the opponent. Often, a player can perform a skill in a drill, but when base runners or batters are added to the mix, he loses focus and thinks more about the opponent than executing the skill. Balls bounce and roll the same way in practice that they do in a game. The game remains the same. The trick is to get players to handle each situation in a game the same way that they deal with it in practice. The more skilled they become in challenging situations, the more confidence they gain in their ability to carry out their responsibilities and just *play the game*. And they have fun doing it!

Recently, the "Next One," NHL hockey star Sidney Crosby said, "I have been practicing since I was four or five years old, but that wasn't really practice. I was just having fun. . . . I just loved to play hockey." That's what the game should be for our players—fun. A by-product of the games approach is that practices become more interesting and, more important, more fun. All our players should be like Crosby. When they say, "Coach, practice was fun today," that is a good thing. We did our job, and they didn't even realize it.

In closing, I'd like to thank those coaches whose passion for the development of baseball inspired me to write this book. Special thanks to Dick Birmingham, Jim Jones, Rodger Grey, Pete Caliendo, Bill Arce, and Charlie Greene. You've kept the game growing—and kept it fun.

Let's play ball!

THROWING GAMES

Four Corners

Age: _All_   Skill Level: _All_

Introduction

Baseball is often considered nothing more than a game of catch. Four Corners focuses on involving the entire team in catching and making accurate throws over the length of the distance between two bases, and forces players to concentrate on catching, throwing mechanics, footwork, and making accurate throws. If players have problems playing this game, they probably should not progress much further until they master it. The object of the game is to move the ball around the four corners of the infield as accurately as possible for a specified number of times.

Equipment

Baseballs, gloves, bases

Setup

- Divide the team into four equal groups.
- Each group assembles at one of the bases and forms a line so that the first person in the line is standing in front of the base straddling the base line. The other players in the line should be at least 10 feet (3 m) behind the first player and facing in the same direction.
- The first player in line should be facing the next base.
- Place all infielders at their respective bases and mix in outfielders and pitchers to even up the lines.
- Place two or three balls safely off to the side near each base.
- The coach should occupy a spot where he can observe best.

Procedure

The coach gives a ball to the first player at home plate. On command, the player steps with his right foot over his left and throws the ball to the player standing at third. After completing the throw, the player hustles to the back of the line and the next person in line takes his place awaiting a throw. When the player at third catches the ball from home, he steps with his right foot over his left and throws to second base. He then hustles to the end of his line. (Before throwing to the next base, left-handed throwers will have to turn their bodies so that the glove-side foot can step in the direction of the next base.) Players follow the same procedure at each succeeding base. The ball continues going around the bases until the coach tells the team to stop. Before starting the game, the coach should give the team a goal. For example, a good goal for a novice team might be to make 20 throws without a mistake. This kind of goal involves them in spurring on their teammates.

Rules: If a player throws the ball over the head or wide of the person to whom he is throwing or it is bobbled or dropped, the ball must be returned to the base from which the bad throw was made and the game starts again from scratch. If a ball is thrown short in the dirt and the receiving player catches it, it counts as a good throw. After three or four times around the bases without a mistake, the coach should call, "Reverse." The player who receives the ball then has to start it going in the opposite direction.

Coaches can think of any number of ways to make this game easier or more difficult. One way to make it harder is to have players do reverse pivots before throwing. For novice groups or players who are not proficient at throwing, shorten the distance between the "corners" to allow the players to have success. The coach can also yell, "Diagonal" when the ball is in the air. When this occurs, the receiving player has to catch and then throw across the diamond to the person in the corner opposite to him.

When teams can make 20 throws without an error, increase the number of throws, increase the distance between throws, or decrease the parameters of what is considered a good throw.

Coaching Points

- Make certain that players step directly toward their target, not across their bodies.
- Emphasize two-handed catches.
- Force players to hop when they make their steps; don't let them just walk through the motions.
- Watch that players are not hurrying to make throws but that they are executing proper arm action.

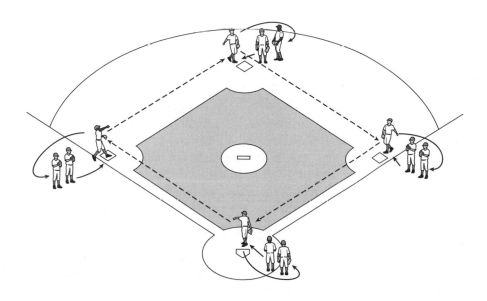

Hit the Target Squarely

Age: *All*   **Skill Level:**

Introduction

If the premise is that baseball is simply a game of catch, then the most important skill in the game is throwing. Too often this skill is overlooked or given short shrift during practice. Teams warm up but pay little attention to the throwing-arm action or the target of their throws. This game forces players to focus on their targets and throw the ball properly. This activity should be the first thing that players do when they begin their throwing warm-ups, and the principles behind it should guide them through the entire prepractice or pregame throwing program. Skills to emphasize here are keeping the eyes on the target, using proper throwing mechanics, and using correct catching technique.

Equipment

Baseballs, gloves

Setup

- Wearing gloves, players pair up and form two lines approximately 30 feet (10 m) apart. Partners face each other.
- Players should be at least 12 feet (3.5 m) away from the next nearest player in their line.
- To start, each player in the first line has a baseball in his glove.

Procedure

On command from the coach, the players holding baseballs follow proper throwing mechanics and throw to their partners in the second line. Players in the second line should begin in position to catch a thrown ball, holding both the glove hand and the throwing hand in front of the body, ready to receive the ball. After catching the ball, players in the second line hold the ball until the coach again gives the command to throw. Players in the first line now assume the catching position. Throwing continues in this manner until the coach thinks that the players have developed sufficiently to play catch on their own without prompts.

Throwers concentrate on throwing to a square on their partner's body—an area roughly 1 foot (30 cm) to either side of the shoulders on the left and right and from the brim of the cap to the center of the chest on the top and bottom (see figure). Players should aim all throws to that target area.

As the players' throwing progresses, the lines should be moved farther apart in 10-foot (3 m) increments. A longer distance increases the difficulty of hitting the target and requires more concentration.

Scoring: Throwers receive a point for each throw in the target area. If the receiver has to reach far left or right or move to catch the ball, the thrower receives no points. Likewise, if the throw is within the target area and is not caught, the receiving player loses a point. Partners should keep track of their score each day. For incentive, the winning player in each tandem could be given reduced clean-up responsibilities at the end of practice or receive some similar benefit.

Coaching Points

- Coaches should watch to make certain that players are using good throwing mechanics.
- With younger players, players could begin on one knee and progress to a standing position.
- Coaches can enhance the throwing game with older players by giving points only for balls thrown to the throwing side of the partner. As the lines become farther apart, hitting the target becomes more difficult.
- Coaches should always be aware of age-specific limits and give players opportunities for success. Pairing players of equal ability provides further opportunities for success.

1.3 ——— **Yoga Toss** ———

Age: *All*   **Skill Level:** *All, especially beginners*

Introduction

To teach the proper arm action for throwing, the best approach is to isolate body parts so that the coach can assess whether players are performing the skill properly. This game involves only the throwing arm and nothing else—no feet, no hips—in teaching the basic arm action of the throw. The game enables coaches to see where the arm action breaks down and creates an environment that allows players to self-examine the action and make corrections.

Equipment

One baseball for each pair of athletes; for younger players, soft rag balls or even tennis balls

Setup

- Divide players into two lines.
- Players pair up and face partners about 10 feet (3 m) away; players should pair up with those of equal skill level.
- Players sit with their legs crossed in front of their bodies in a yoga position, as if they were meditating.
- No gloves are necessary for this game; players perform barehanded.

Procedure

To start, pick one of the lines to be the throwers—these players will each have a baseball. The players in the other line are the receivers.

Before starting the game, coaches should explain and show the correct way to hold the ball and demonstrate proper arm action. Emphasis should be given to the grip and pressure of the hand on the ball and the relationship of the ball to the fingers. (Many excellent texts show proper grip and throwing action.)

The game begins with the thrower having both hands together and the ball in his throwing hand. On command of the coach, the player takes the ball down, back, and away from his bare glove hand (see figure). He makes a big circle with his arm and the ball and then throws the ball softly to his receiver, aiming for the receiver's chest. The player's head should remain still, and his eyes should be on his target throughout the throwing motion. The receiver catches the ball with both hands and then waits for a command from the coach to throw the ball back to his partner in the same manner. Coaches should walk behind both lines of players and watch closely for coaching points while they are giving commands. When they spot mechanical flaws, coaches can easily stop a player, point out the flaw, and move the player's arm or hand into the correct position. To increase focus, throwers can score points when the thrown ball hits the chest target.

An additional benefit to this game is that by not using gloves, receivers focus on using two hands to catch the ball.

Coaching Points

- The player's hand should be on top of the ball throughout the throwing motion until the release point.
- The wrist and hand should be loose and bent, not stiff.
- The elbow remains bent through the motion and is shoulder height or higher at release.
- The arm motion should be continuous and relaxed. The player should not hesitate during any part of the motion.
- The elbow must remain bent as the ball is taken away from the nonthrowing hand. The elbow must not lock up to create a straight arm during the takeaway.
- The head should not move.
- After release, the arm should follow through in the direction of the throw. Players must not snap the ball and stop their arms from continuing.

One-Knee Throwing

Age: *All*   Skill Level: *All*

Introduction

This game builds on the skills started in Yoga Toss (page 6). With younger players, this should be the second stage of the throwing process. With more advanced players, this game might be the starting point for teaching throwing. Although players may have been playing the game for years, this stage provides an excellent review. The objective remains the same—teaching correct arm action—but One-Knee Throwing adds the upper body, lead arm, and follow-through to the throwing mix.

Equipment

Baseballs, gloves

Setup

- Divide players into two groups.
- Players pair up and face their partners about 15 to 20 feet (5 to 6 m) away; players of equal skill level should be paired together.
- Players bend down and kneel on the knee of the throwing-arm side.
- They point the glove-side foot toward the partner.

Procedure

Again, before starting the game, coaches should explain and demonstrate proper arm action from the kneeling position. Emphasis here should be on the rotational movement of the upper body, the position of the glove-side shoulder, and the follow-through.

The game begins with the throwers having both hands together in the center of the body and gripping the ball properly in the throwing hand inside the glove. All the balls should be in the same line at the start. On command of the coach, the throwers rotate the upper body away from their partners while pulling the throwing hand and ball away from the glove as they rotate. The players then take the throwing arm down, back, and away from the body in the same circular motion that they used in Yoga Toss. The difference in this game is that the upper body rotates at the hips and the glove-side shoulder points toward the receiver while the arm moves into release position. This game introduces the concept of keeping the front side of the body closed. After the ball has been released, the throwing arm should continue toward the receiver and the upper body should rotate in the opposite direction. At finish, the throwing shoulder should be close to the player's chin and the throwing arm should be outside the player's glove-side knee.

Players can again compete against each other by keeping track of the number of times the throws hit the target area. Receivers must also use two hands whenever catching.

A good visual tool to help players see whether they are throwing correctly is a strip of electrical tape placed around the circumference of the baseball and across the seams. When players hold the ball, they should place the thumb on the tape on the bottom of the ball and spread the fingers so that they are touching the edges of the tape on top of the ball. If they throw the ball properly, they can see the tape as a straight line like the hands of a clock from 12 to 6. If they throw improperly, the tape will wobble on the throw.

Scoring: Points can be scored whenever the ball is thrown into the target area—the receiver's chest area from shoulder to shoulder and midchest to the brim of the cap.

Coaching Points

- Don't allow players to sit on their haunches.
- The wrist and hand should be loose and bent, not stiff.
- The front shoulder should not rotate too much. Excessive rotation leads to other throwing faults.
- Make certain that the elbow remains bent through the motion and is shoulder height or higher at release.
- The throwing arm should continue forward and finish outside the glove-side knee.
- Watch ball rotation.

1.5

Whoosh

Age: *All* **Skill Level:** *All, especially beginners*

Introduction

This game—learned from Gil Patterson of the Oakland A's—takes its name from the sound made when a 24-inch-long (60 cm) dowel is used in place of a ball for proper throwing action. This drill is useful for players who have difficulty understanding the path that the arm should follow in the throwing motion. Taking the ball out of the equation allows focus on the arm path (the process) instead of where the ball is going (the outcome). In a few simple steps, which feature concrete stimuli, players can actually feel the proper throwing motion.

Equipment

A dowel 24 inches (60 cm) long and 3/8 inch (1 cm) in diameter for each player, taped on the end that will be held in the hand

Setup

- Throwers stand in a circle spaced far enough apart that they will not hit each other.
- The coach stands in the middle of the circle so that he can observe players' arm actions.

Procedure

This game evolves through several stages to simulate the stages of learning how to throw. Sample commands for which numbers can be substituted are placed in parenthesis. In the first stage, players use only their arms and stand flat-footed. The idea is to isolate the throwing action from the actions of the body. On command (hands together!), players stand with their feet shoulder-width apart and hold their hands together in front of their chests. On the second command (throwing position!), players take both arms out to the sides of their bodies like those of a conductor directing an orchestra. The dowel is held like the conductor's baton. On the next command (scratch your back!), players take the throwing arm toward the head so that the dowel is in a position to scratch their backs between the upper regions of scapula bones (this gets the arm into the classic L position). At the same time, the non-throwing arm moves to the area in front of and away from the chest. On the last command (throw!), players quickly move the throwing arm forward as if throwing a ball, trying to make the dowel "whoosh" out in front of their bodies. To make a loud noise with the dowel, players have to snap the wrist at the release point.

In the second stage of Whoosh, coaches use the same commands, but players now turn their bodies so that they are perpendicular to their stance in the first stage. On the second command, the players should be conscious of using the lead arm as a sighting arm, much like an archer. On the final command, players should step toward an imaginary target while snapping their dowels in imitation of throwing.

The third and final stage involves the entire body in the throwing motion. Players begin in a relaxed position with their hands together as if they had just received a thrown ball. On "One," they should rotate the throwing foot outward 90 degrees so that the instep faces their imaginary receiver. On "Two," as the arms move into throwing position, the upper body rotates and the glove foot steps toward the target. The third command remains the same. On "Four," players execute the throwing motion by snapping the dowel in front of the body, making sure to follow through so that the dowel finishes outside the glove-side leg.

Coaches should walk around the inside of the circle throughout these stages watching each player's movements carefully and pointing out flaws in delivery. The freeze command discussed in the introduction is useful in this activity. Whenever the coach calls, "Freeze," players should check themselves for proper technique.

After 5 to 10 mock "whoosh" throws at each stage, players pair off, replace the dowels with baseballs, and go through same four steps, this time actually throwing to their partners. After 5 to 10 throws with oral commands from the coach, players can throw and catch on their own until they are warmed up. Again, the element of competition can be introduced and a scoring system can be devised.

Coaching Points

- Emphasize keeping the elbows and wrists bent. Watch out for straight arms.
- The wrist and hand should be loose and bent, not stiff.
- At release, the wrist should snap in front of the body, creating a whooshing sound with the dowel. The faster the dowel moves through the air, the louder the "whoosh."
- The glove-side foot should be pointed at the target.

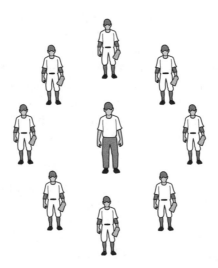

Touch 'Em All

Age: *8 and older*   **Skill Level:** ⚾⚾

Introduction

Although this is an excellent game to use with younger players to hone their throwing skills while also improving baserunning and hitting, it can also be a fun and challenging game for older players. Its objective is to teach players to make accurate throws to each base without hurrying—thereby cutting down on errors. With younger players use a field of an age-appropriate size.

Equipment

Baseballs (regulation or softies), batting tee, cones or extra set of bases

Setup

- Place cones, or extra bases if they are available, about 3 feet (1 m) outside and 3 feet farther from home plate than the normal distance.
- Divide the team in half; one is at bat and the other is in the field.
- Players on defense assume normal field positions.
- One batter is in the batter's box, and the rest of the offensive players are in a line safely removed from home plate.

Procedure

Place the ball on the batting tee. The first batter hits the ball on the tee and begins to run if he hits the ball in fair territory. The objective of the batter is to run around the cones near each base and continue to home without stopping.

After the ball is hit, the defense must field the ball or chase it down and throw to each base in any order as long as the final throw goes to home plate. The fielder who catches the throw must touch the base before throwing to the next base. If the runner beats the ball to home plate, the offense is awarded a point. An out is recorded when the defense gets the ball to home before the runner reaches home.

A ball caught in the air is not an automatic out. The defensive players must still throw the ball around the infield to each base. For example, if a batter hits a ball to the left fielder, he must field the ball and then throw it back into the infield. If the throw goes to third base, the third baseman would touch third and then throw to second or first. That fielder in turn would catch, touch the base, and throw to another base as yet untouched before the final throw goes home.

No bunting or sliding is allowed in the game. After three outs, teams switch sides. Coaches should switch defensive positions often to give players experience at each position. With older players, coaches could use flip toss instead of a batting tee.

When played often, the game teaches players to keep their composure and helps them avoid the kind of play that results in multiple errors that often plagues youth games.

Coaching Points

⊙ The nature of the game dictates that players hit ground balls or line drives to be successful.

⊙ A common mistake that players make is rushing their throws before their bodies are in position to throw. Coaches should pay close attention to fielders to make sure that they are getting their bodies underneath them before they throw.

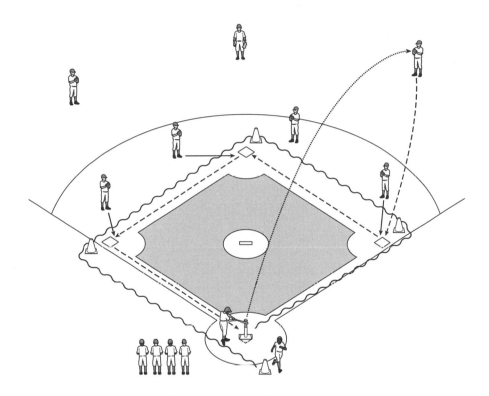

Doubles

Age: _8 and older_   **Skill Level:**

Introduction

Similar to Touch 'Em All (page 12), this game is fun to use with younger players to improve their throwing skills and mechanics. It is also a good throwing warm-up game for older players because it incorporates many of the skills required for Four Corners (page 2) and adds runners into the mix. The goal is to have players make accurate throws without focusing on the distraction of the runner; in other words, it teaches players to play the game, not the opponent. As with the other games, when playing with younger players use an age-appropriate-sized field.

Equipment

Baseballs (regulation or softies), batting tee, cones or extra set of bases, home plate

Setup

- Place two cones, or extra bases if they are available, about 3 feet (1 m) outside and 3 feet farther from home plate than the normal distance at first and second bases.
- Divide the team in half; one is at bat and the other is in the field.
- Players on defense assume normal positions in fair territory. If fewer than nine players are available per team, position players accordingly.
- One batter is in the batter's box, and the rest of the offensive players are in a line safely removed from home plate.

Procedure

The ball is placed on the batting tee or flip tossed from the side by a coach. If the ball is hit into fair territory, the batter runs around the cone at first base and continues past the cone at second base. If the batter–runner beats the ball to second base, the offense scores a point.

When the ball is hit into fair territory, the defense must field, catch, or chase down the ball and then make three throws. When one of the defensive players catches the ball, he must touch the base before throwing to the next base. The last throw must go to second base. A defensive player can handle the ball only once during each at-bat. An out is recorded when the defense gets the ball to second base before the runner passes the second-base cone. A ball caught in the air is not an automatic out; the defense must still make three throws. Players cannot hand off the ball to someone else. They must throw it.

No bunting or sliding is allowed in the game. After three outs, teams switch sides. Coaches should switch defensive positions often to give players experience at each position.

After three outs or after each player has batted, switch sides and resume play with the defense now on offense. Games of three or four innings work best. Have players sprint on and off the field to speed up play.

With older players, the flip toss is preferred. Other variations would be to require more than three throws or require that one of the throws be to first or third base before throwing to second.

Coaching Points

- As with Touch 'Em All, coaches should pay close attention to fielders to make sure they are getting their bodies underneath them before throwing. Failure to do so is a good indicator that they are rushing their throws.

- Coaches should insist that outfielders use good crow hop technique on the longer throws.

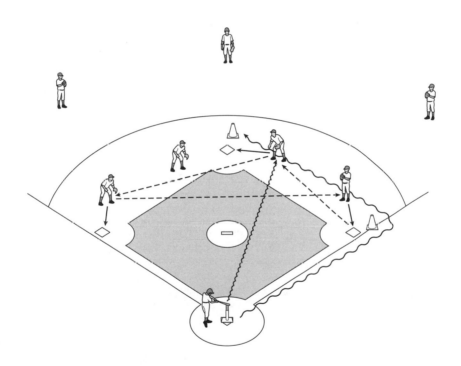

Progressive Long Toss

Age: *All*   **Skill Level:** 🔵🔵

Introduction

Much has been written and said about the benefits of long toss. Several schools of thought exist on the issue. The following game is a version of long toss that can be used with players of all ages. Besides slowly working players up to longer throws in its progression, it forces players to be accurate and adjust their throws based on their location and distance from a target area. The game is an excellent prepractice warm-up to get the team into a competitive mode.

Equipment

Baseballs, gloves

Setup

- ◎ Two players serve as catcher near home plate. The two players chosen should be the best throwers on the team.
- ◎ Divide the remaining players into two lines that stretch from foul line to foul line across the field. The second line should be 15 feet (5 m) behind the first line. Players should be spread out evenly on the field so that half throw to one catcher and the other half throw to the second catcher. Divide lines by ability level keeping the more skilled players on one side of the field.
- ◎ The distance of the lines from home plate will depend on the age and ability level of the players. For younger players, the first line should only be about 60 feet from home plate at the start.

Procedure

After players are sufficiently warm, each catcher throws a ball to the first person in the first line on his side of the field. The player makes a return throw to the catcher. Immediately after receiving the ball, the catcher throws a ball to the first person in the second line, who also immediately makes a return throw. Then the catcher throws to the second person in the first row, then to the second person in the second row, and so on until all players have had a throw.

After all players have thrown, players switch positions so that the players in the nearer line move to the back line and vice versa. Throwing continues in this fashion for as many throws as the coach deems necessary.

After a few rotations, both lines move back 15 feet (5 m) and another round of throwing begins until the maximum distance the coach desires is reached. The following table shows maximum distances to use with various age groups.

Age	Maximum distance
Under 12	70–135 feet (20–40 m)
12–15	90–170 feet (25–50 m)
16 and over	170–250 feet (50–75 m)

Also, depending on the distance and ability level, players can either throw on the fly or use one-bounce throws.

Scoring of the game can be done in several ways. One method is to mark an area around the catcher with cones. Throws within the area score a point; those outside the area don't count. Another way to score is to add the element of time to the game. The first group to finish their throwing progression in the manner that the coach describes wins the contest. The main goal, however, should be accuracy not speed.

Coaching Point

◉ Pay close attention to throwing mechanics of players, especially at the longer distances. If mechanics change radically, the player may not be strong enough to throw the increased distance and should not be allowed to do so.

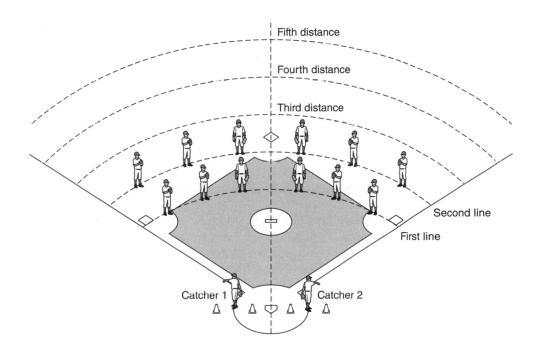

Four Corners Against the Clock

Age: *12 and older*   **Skill Level:** 🔵🔵🔵🔵

Introduction

"He was out by a step!" How many times in the history of baseball has that phrase been said? Although the expression is somewhat true, it is also inaccurate. When a close play occurs and a runner is out, a more precise statement would be "Wow! He was out by a 10th of a second!" Baseball is a game of quick bursts followed by pauses. When players field or catch a ball, they can't hang on to it. They have to do something with it—and quickly! This game is essentially the same as Four Corners (page 2) with the dimension of quickness added to accuracy. It teaches players to get the ball out of the glove quickly after catching it, to get their feet and bodies into throwing position rapidly, and to make firm, fast throws to the next base.

Equipment

Baseballs, gloves, bases, stopwatch

Setup

- Team should be divided into groups as in Four Corners.
- Each group occupies positions near one of the bases.

Procedure

This game uses the same rules as Four Corners, but instead of trying to reach a certain number of throws, a team tries to see how many throws and catches they can make in a given period. This goal focuses attention on both accuracy and quickness. When bad throws occur in this game, the player who made the error has to shag the ball. Because quickness may force errant throws, a premium is placed on fielding in this game. The fielder, by being quick on his feet or with his hands, can save the thrower the work of having to chase down the bad throw and the game can continue uninterrupted. Coaches should start the stopwatch when the first throw is made and then count how many throws are made in a given period. When a throw is errant and not caught, the ball goes back to the point of origination of the bad throw and the game continues.

Encourage a team to beat their previous best each time they play this game. To start, the team can play a game of Four Corners. Then, before moving to another part of practice, the coach can get out the stopwatch and challenge the team to see how many throws they can make in a 30- or 60-second period. If the team is dissatisfied with their performance for a day, coaches won't have to tell them to do it again. They will want to!

Coaching Points

● Make certain that players step directly toward their target, not across their bodies. In their haste, players sometimes forget mechanics and force bad throws with bad mechanics.

● Watch that players move their feet quickly when throwing. Quick feet lead to quicker throws.

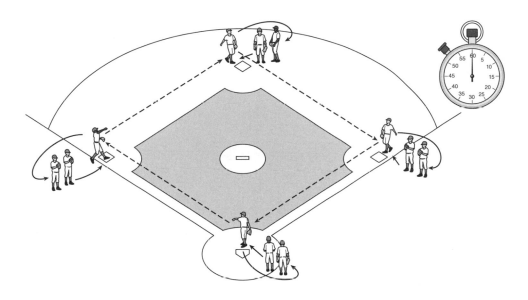

1.10 Globetrotter

Age: *12 and older*   **Skill Level:** ◉◉◉◉

Introduction

Everyone is familiar with the wizardry that the Harlem Globetrotters display in their shows. This zesty game imitates their routine and adapts it for baseball. When performed as a pregame warm-up, it can even be intimidating to the opposition. Although challenging, especially for younger players, when completed successfully it can create a sense of team pride and accomplishment. The goal of the game is develop dexterity and a quick release in the throwing motion.

Equipment

Baseballs, gloves, bases, four cones, stopwatch

Setup

- Place a cone in the baseline 10 feet (3 m) to the right of second base and another in the baseline 10 feet to the left of second.
- Place two cones 10 feet to either side home plate.
- Divide the team into two equal groups. Each group should then be subdivided into three subgroups.
- One subgroup occupies positions at the cone to the left of home plate, third base, and the cone to the left of second; the other subgroup occupies positions at the cone to the right of home plate, first base, and the cone to the right of second.

Procedure

The first player in each line at the home plate cones starts with a ball. On the coach's command, players throw balls in the following manner: One ball goes from the right-field side of home to first base to the right-field side of second and then back to the right-field side of home; the other ball goes from the left-field side of home to third base to the left-field side of second and then back to the left-field side of home. Throws only go in a triangle instead of a square as in Four Corners (page 2).

The coach can yell, "Reverse" at any time to reverse the direction of the ball. When a ball is misthrown, both the catcher and the receiver have to chase it down and run it back to the spot of the error before play can continue.

Especially with younger players, care must be taken so that the lines at home plate and the lines at second base are not too close or in a direct path with each other.

One side of the infield competes against the other in this game. Scoring can be done in numerous ways. One would be to use a stopwatch and count the number of throws that each side makes in two minutes. Another would be to see which group reaches a predetermined number of throws first.

Coaching Points

● Make certain that players step directly toward their target, not across their bodies. In their haste, players sometimes forget mechanics and force bad throws with bad mechanics.

● Watch that players move their feet quickly when throwing. Quick footwork leads to quicker throws.

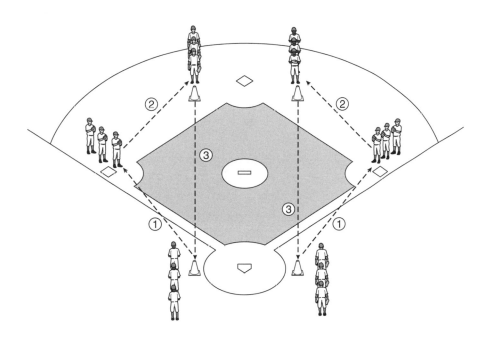

1.11 — Stars

Age: *12 and older*   **Skill Level:** ⚾⚾⚾⚾

Introduction

This variation of Four Corners (page 2) incorporates more of the throws that players actually use in a game. The progression of throws mimics many of the crucial situations that could occur in a contest—for example, the steal of second or the first-and-third double steal. The game also gives teams practice in oral communication and could serve as a good warm-up throwing drill before pregame infield practice. It takes its name from the fact a diagram of the throws being made looks like a lopsided five-pointed star on paper.

Equipment

Baseballs, gloves, bases

Setup

- A first baseman and third baseman are stationed at their respective bases.
- A second baseman and shortstop are at double-play depth near second base.
- A catcher is in down position behind home plate.
- Additional infielders are on the outfield grass or in foul territory near their positions.
- The coach stands in the infield about 20 feet (6 m) in front of home plate.

Procedure

The coach begins the game by tossing the ball to the catcher crouched behind home plate. The second baseman breaks to cover second as soon as the coach tosses the ball. The catcher throws to the second baseman covering second as he would on a straight steal. The second baseman receives the ball, practices a V tag on an imaginary runner, quickly reverse pivots, and throws to third. The third baseman makes a fake tag, executes a reverse pivot, and then fires to the first baseman, who tags the base as he would on a putout at first. Immediately after the stretch and tag, the first baseman fires to the shortstop covering second and yells, "Tag" to execute a double play with no force at second. The shortstop executes a tag on an imaginary runner and then wheels and throws to home, where the catcher blocks the plate and executes a tag. He then tosses the ball to the second catcher, who has assumed a down position behind home plate, and the throwing routine begins again.

As soon as each infielder has made his throw, with the exception of the catcher, he gets out of the infield and the next person in line replaces him. Before the throws are made, all participants should yell commands that would be shouted in a game. When the second baseman is making the tag, everyone should yell, "Three" in unison to let the player know where to throw. When the third baseman is tagging, everyone yells, "One," and so on.

Use a stopwatch for this game and challenge the infielders to make as many throws as possible in one minute without a miscue. An errant throw or missed catch means that the game starts over. Another way to make this a challenging game is to have two sets of infielders each going against the stopwatch. When one group finishes, the time is noted, and then the next group gets a turn. Teams could play best-of-three or best-of-five matches. Variations of the patterns of throws could also be incorporated. Instead of throwing to second, for example, the catcher could throw to the shortstop, who could throw to first as if executing a double play. The first baseman could throw to the third baseman, who would then throw to the second baseman, who would return the ball home, completing the star. Of course, oral commands would have to be altered.

Coaching Points

- Watch that players are not simply hurrying to make throws but are also executing proper arm action.
- Make certain that if the first baseman is right-handed, he steps in the direction of the pitcher's mound before throwing to second. This way he is practicing not throwing the ball directly on line with a runner going from first to second.
- Force players to hop when they make their steps; don't let them just walk through the motions.

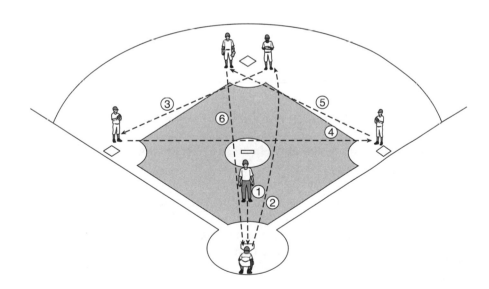

1.12 — Soft Hands

Age: *High school and older*   **Skill Level:** ⚾⚾⚾⚾

Introduction

In all of baseball history, probably no one was faster than Brian Doyle when it came to transferring the ball from the glove to the throwing hand on a double-play pivot and getting rid of it. The second baseman, who played briefly for the Yankees and the Athletics, made it seem as if the ball never touched the glove on the play. Although they may never be as quick as Doyle was, infielders need to be able to get rid of the ball quickly to make a double play possible. The aim of this game is to help infielders develop soft hands—an inside term for the ability to field and throw so smoothly that everything looks relaxed and natural—by practicing transferring the ball from glove to hand rather than catching it. This makes the act of fielding and catching look smooth and unhurried, especially on double-play pivots.

Equipment

One baseball for each pair of athletes; Softhands or other foam-type catching device

Setup

- Divide infielders into two lines on the infield dirt or outfield grass.
- Infielders pair up and face their partners about 40 feet (12 m) away; players of equal skill level should be paired together.
- Infielders wear Softhands instead of their fielder's gloves.

Procedure

After players assume their positions on the field, the coach gives the command to start throwing. Because of the nature of the Softhands device, players cannot catch the ball but can only transfer it from the glove hand to the throwing hand. Infielders must receive the throw with both hands in the thumbs-together, fingers-up position and immediately turn the glove hand to transfer the ball to the throwing hand. Because the nature of the foam glove does not allow the ball to be caught and held, another benefit of this game is that it reinforces catching with two hands.

After making the "catch," the infielder immediately transforms his body and feet from catching position into throwing position and make a return throw to his partner. The game continues in this fashion for 3 to 5 minutes. During the last 30 seconds, the players should try to pick up the speed of the game and move into a rapid-fire mode.

Coaches can challenge players by using a stopwatch and then having the players see how many catches and throws they can make in a one-minute period. They can also make the game more difficult by having receivers hop over an imaginary sliding runner before they make their return throw.

Coaching Points

- Make sure that players keep their hands together when preparing to receive the ball.
- Fingers should be pointed up, wrists should be relaxed, and elbows should be bent.
- Watch that infielders give with the ball when they catch it. They have to bring their arms in toward their bodies as they make the transfer. Failure to do so will cause the ball to bounce off the soft glove.
- Players should also transfer their feet quickly into throwing position as they make the catch.
- Be certain that fielders use good arm action on their throws, especially during the rapid-fire mode. Sometimes players start to push the ball in an effort to complete the drill.

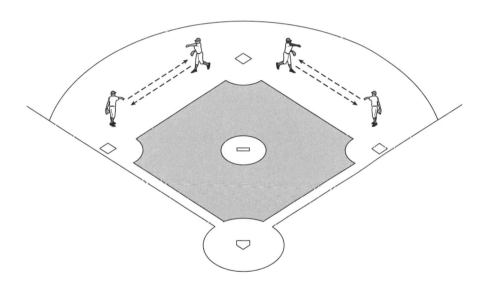

Cutoff and Relay Throw Race

Age: *12 and older* **Skill Level:** ⚾⚾⚾⚾

Introduction

When the news was released that a well-known major league outfielder had converted to an evangelical faith, a cynical fan was heard to say, "How could he find religion? He couldn't even hit the cutoff man!" Few things irritate coaches more than an outfielder's throw that misses a cutoff man and allows runners to advance extra bases. This game involves the entire team and creates a competitive environment that can vastly improve cutoff and relays skills.

Equipment

Baseballs, gloves

Setup

- The team should be divided into three equal groups of six players each.
- Ideally, each group should have an equal number of catchers, pitchers, infielders, and outfielders.
- Each group should form a line from home plate to about 15 feet (5 m) from the outfield fence. Players should be spaced at intervals along the line according to the following:
  - → Always have a catcher as the first person in line (player 1) behind home plate. Player 2 should be a first baseman or third baseman who stands about 65 feet (20 m) away. Then station an infielder (player 3) about 65 feet farther away. The other players should be spaced about 50 feet (15 m) apart from this point.
- The distances can be adjusted depending on the age and ability of the players.
- For teams that do not have a fence on their practice field, a coach should become the seventh person in line.
- If 18 players aren't available, teams can play this game with two lines by slightly adjusting the spacing.

Procedure

Throw-down bases, home plates, or even gloves should be used as substitutes for home plate. Use the diamond's home plate for the middle line and place the other two home plates 15 feet to the left and right of it. The game begins with a ball in the hand of each of the catchers. On the coach's "go" command, the catchers throw to the player closest to them. That player signals for the ball by waving his hands back and forth above his head and making some verbal call. (This oral signal can be at the coach's discretion. "Here, here" or "Ball, ball" are suggestions.) This process continues through the first five players in the same manner so that each player has to catch and throw the ball as it travels away from home plate. When the second-to-last player in line throws the ball, he should aim at player 6, but that player does not catch it. Instead, he allows it to go past him and hit the fence behind him. He then sprints to the ball, scoops it up, turns, crow hops, and executes a throw. On the return throws, however, only every other player in line handles the ball. So when the outfielder throws the ball, he skips over player 5 and throws to player 4 instead. Player 4 catches and throws to player 2, etc. The relay ends when the catcher's glove hits the ground in faking a tag at home plate.

The premium here is on making quick and accurate throws—throws that are on line and have some velocity.

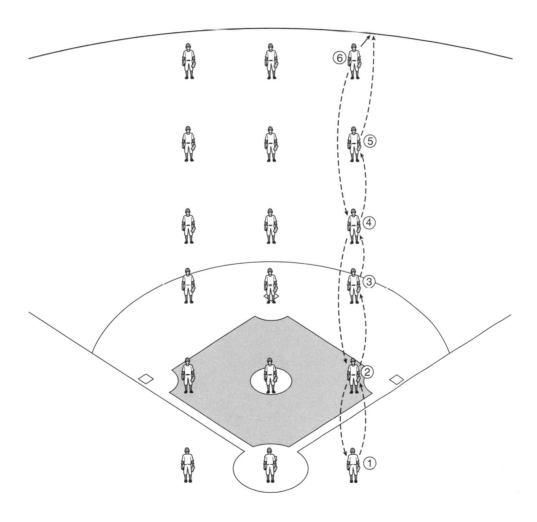

(continued)

(continued)

Usually, this game should be a double-elimination contest to give teams a chance to make up for a poor performance. To give the team some tactical experience, the coach can let each line decide the order in which players line up. This allows them the opportunity to position players according to arm strength or accuracy.

Coaching Points

- Watch to be certain that players in a relay team signal with their arms for the ball.
- Make certain that when the ball is in the air, the player to whom it is being thrown turns his body so that his glove-hand shoulder is perpendicular to the player to whom he will throw it after the catch. This way the body is already in position to throw, speeding up the process of the relay.
- Emphasize two-handed catches.
- Check to be sure that players use their voices as well as their arms when signaling for the ball.

CHAPTER

2

INFIELD GAMES

Backhand Force

Age: *12 and older*   **Skill Level:** ●●●●●

Introduction

The Wizard of Oz, Cardinals Hall of Fame shortstop Ozzie Smith, made it look easy—going into the hole behind third, backhanding the ball, planting or sometimes jumping, and then zipping the ball to second base to get the force on the lead runner. Although he made it look easy, the reality was that it was a difficult play, and one that Smith practiced regularly. This game gives players an opportunity to work on this difficult but important throwing skill. When a ball is hit deep in the hole, the average shortstop may not have a strong enough arm to throw out the batter at first base. But if a runner is on first when the ball is hit, the shortstop may be able to make the force play at second base and get an out.

Equipment

Gloves, balls, bases, four cones

Setup

- Mark spots with lining chalk on the infield where the shortstop and second baseman should stand when at double-play depth.
- Place second basemen at double-play depth on the infield.
- Shortstops stand in a line at double-play depth.
- Place four cones 3 to 4 feet (1 to 1.2 m) apart at various spots in the infield hole behind third base. Place the cones so that cone 1 is closest to the shortstop and cone 4 is farthest away.

Procedure

The first shortstop, with a ball in his glove, assumes his ready position at double-play depth in the infield on the spot marked with chalk. On command of the coach or another player, the shortstop sprints to the first cone, simulates fielding a ball at that spot, and then turns and throws to the second baseman, who has assumed a pivot position at second base. After the throw, the next shortstop assumes his position at the mark and performs the same routine. After each shortstop has completed the first throw, the game continues with shortstops sprinting to cones 2, 3, and 4 in succession.

By starting with the ball already in the glove, the fielder needs to concentrate only on getting his body set and making the throw to the base. Placing the cones farther from the fielder or at various locations from the front of the infield to the outfield grass will make the game more challenging. As players become adept at making this throw, the cones should be rearranged to add difficulty. The game can be scored based on the accuracy of the throws and the quickness of the fielder in transferring from fielding to throwing position.

Coaching Points

- Make certain that shortstops field the ball with their throwing-side foot forward, which enables them to break their momentum, plant, turn, and throw more quickly.
- Fielding with the glove-side foot forward forces fielders to take an additional step before throwing.

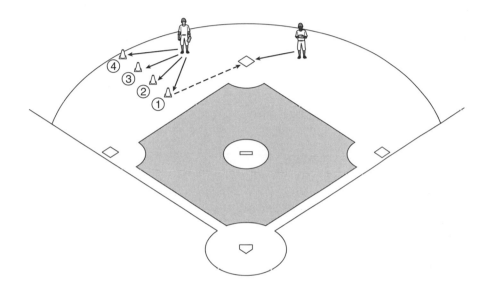

2.2 — **Balls in the Dirt**

Age: *High school and older*   **Skill Level:** ⚾⚾⚾⚾

Introduction

Although players are sometimes chosen to play first base because they are tall or slow, first basemen still need to be athletic to play the position well. Fielding errant throws in the dirt takes good eye–hand coordination and quickness. First basemen need constant practice in this skill to become adept in its execution. This game enables a coach to provide adequate practice in fielding balls in the dirt and accurately measure the abilities of the team's first basemen.

Equipment

Pitching machine, gloves, balls, bases

Setup

- First basemen assemble at first base.
- Set up a pitching machine near the mound about 65 feet (20 m) from first base. The machine should be set to throw a ball approximately 75 miles per hour (120 km/h).
- A shagger for return throws from the fielders stands off to the side near the pitching machine.

Procedure

One player assumes a position at first base ready to catch a ball thrown by the pitching machine. The coach or feeder should raise a ball in his hand as if to throw it and then set it into the pitching machine. Doing this helps the fielder follow the ball more clearly. The machine should be set so that the feeder can easily manipulate the direction of the ball up and down, sometimes throwing the ball in the dirt and sometimes making a good throw. This approach gives the fielder gamelike practice because the accuracy of the throws is unpredictable. Even if the machine is not moved, however, no two balls will bounce exactly the same way, so the first basemen will get a variety of bounces. Also, by adjusting the direction of the machine slightly, first basemen can be given work on backhanding and forehanding balls or scooping balls thrown right at them.

For safety, advise the first basemen not to throw the ball back toward the pitching machine and have the shaggers stand well away from the machine. For scoring, players might be given 20 balls each and earn a point for each handled cleanly. Increasing the speed of the ball out of the machine increases the degree of difficulty of the game and adds to the challenge.

Coaching Points

- Watch that first basemen don't stretch too early, which limits their ability to react to bad hops or errant throws.
- Teach first basemen to catch the ball on the short hop.
- If they sense that the ball will take an in-between hop, have them stand upright and not stretch as much. This stance prevents them from being eaten up by the ball.

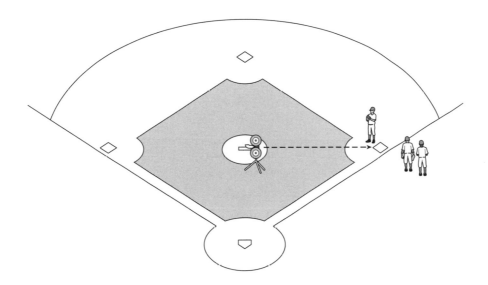

Crossover

Age: *All*   Skill Level: *All*

Introduction

On balls hit sharply to either side, the infielder will not have time to circle the ball. Instead, the fielder must with a great burst of energy make a crossover step, try to get to the ball, and field it on the backhand or forehand side. This game gives players opportunities to work on the footwork necessary for the crossover step. It also sharpens their reaction skills. Players should become adept at crossing over, breaking down into fielding position, funneling the ball, and transferring into throwing mode.

Equipment

Cones, bucket of baseballs

Setup

- Place two cones 15 to 20 feet (5 to 6 m) apart on the infield dirt according to the ability and age of the players involved.
- The coach should serve as the feeder.
- Infielders line up outside one of the cones.

Procedure

The coach assumes a position about 10 feet (3 m) in front of the cones, facing the players. The first player in line gets into ready position inside one of the cones. (Play can start inside either cone. If the game starts inside the left cone, players will have to cross over to their left side to make the play. The opposite is true if the game starts inside the right cone.) The coach rolls a ball toward the opposite cone. The player reacts, uses a crossover step, gets to the ball, and fields it. After fielding, the player fakes a throw and then sprints to the coach. He places the ball in the bucket and returns to the end of the fielding line. As soon as the first player fields the ball and simulates the throw, the next player in line steps inside the area marked by the cones and assumes a ready position. The coach rolls another ball. When all players have fielded to one side, the line moves to the other cone. Play continues as the coach rolls balls in the opposite direction.

The coach should do the feeding in this game for consistency of speed. Balls should not be rolled so hard that the players have to dive for them. The object of this game is to gain facility in making the crossover step, breaking down, and getting the body in position to throw.

This game can be scored individually or as a team. For example, the coach could set a goal of the number of ground balls to be fielded without an error, say 30. If the infielders reach the goal, the team can proceed to the next part of practice. If they make an error, play starts from scratch. Play continues as long as the coach deems necessary.

Coaching Points

- Occasionally roll balls directly to the fielder to prevent them from cheating to one side or the other.
- Closely watch footwork after fielding to see whether the players are getting their feet under their bodies before throwing.

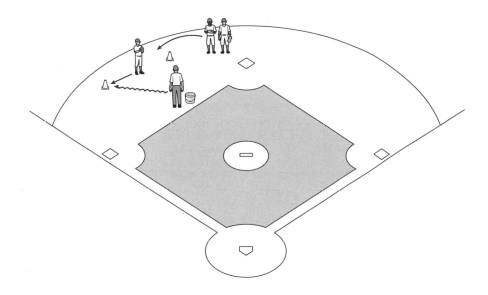

Double-Play Rotation

Age: *12 and older*   **Skill Level:** 🔵🔵🔵🔵

Introduction

Although no one alive today saw them play and little exists on film to substantiate the claims, the lore surrounding the famed Tinkers to Evers to Chance double-play combination for the Cubs in the early 20th century is well known in baseball circles and its celebration in verse must mean that they were pretty good. A great double-play combination has to have a level of comfort to perform at a high level. The shortstop has to know where his second baseman likes to receive the ball and vice versa. This game gives daily opportunities for middle infielders to find that level.

Equipment

Baseballs, one throw-down base

Setup

- Second basemen and shortstops assume double-play depth on the field.
- The coach or a feeder assumes a position on the infield grass between second base and the pitcher's mound.
- Place throw-down base three-fourths of the way between second and first base.
- First basemen assume a position near the throw-down base.

Procedure

The coach or feeder, the shortstop, and the second baseman form a triangle on the field. All the rotation in this game occurs around this triangle. Because middle infielders may play those positions interchangeably, this game provides an opportunity for them to do so. The game works best with several players at each position, but it can also work with only one player at each position.

The game begins with the feeder rolling a ground ball directly at the shortstop. The shortstop fields the ball, bends his right knee toward the ground, and flips to the second baseman covering second. The second baseman should not move into the pivot position until the feeder rolls the ball. After receiving the toss from the shortstop, the second baseman executes a pivot and throws to the first baseman. After the shortstop flips to second, he rotates to the back of the line at second base. After making the pivot and throwing, the second baseman rotates to the line behind the feeder or coach, and the player immediately in line behind the feeder rotates to the shortstop position. First basemen should take turns receiving throws.

The feeder then rolls another ball toward the shortstop, and play continues. Feeders should throw ground balls in succession left and right of the fielders, slower or faster, or even directly behind second base. The key is to give players multiple opportunities to field the types of balls that they may get in a game.

After all the possibilities have been covered at the shortstop position, the feeder should then roll balls to the second basemen in the same fashion. The second basemen work on their feeds to the shortstops covering the base, and the shortstops work on their pivots.

Shortening the throws to first base helps the middle infielders concentrate on feeds and pivots, not the speed of their throws to first. By providing many varieties of throws in a short time, the game helps infielders become more comfortable with each other.

Coaches can devise a myriad of scoring systems for this game. Points can be given for getting feeds chest high and over the base, for example, or taken away on bad tosses.

Coaching Points

- Second basemen should circle the base somewhat and approach it more from the center-field side.
- Teach only a few of the many pivots available and let players decide which one they are more comfortable with.

Enhanced Crossover

2.5

Age: *10 and older*   **Skill Level:** *All*

Introduction

This version of Crossover (page 34) is a bit harder than the original. Because the distance is greater, fielders get practice not only in improving their footwork but also in reading the ball off the bat. And because the ball will be rolling over the uneven surface of the infield, players will have to adjust to the unpredictable hops generated by the pitching machine.

Equipment

Pitching machine, bucket of baseballs, cone

Setup

- A first baseman takes position at first base.
- Place a pitching machine at home plate.
- Infielders line up in the outfield near the shortstop position.
- Place a cone on the dirt portion of the infield where the shortstop should be positioned.

Procedure

Set the pitching machine so that it throws ground balls about 20 to 30 feet (6 to 9 m) to the third-base side of the cone. Adjust the distance based on the age and ability of the players. The first player in line moves in front of the cone and takes a ready position. The coach feeds a ball into the pitching machine. The player reacts, uses a crossover step, gets to the ball, fields it, and throws to first base. As soon as the first player fields the ball and throws, the next player moves in front of the cone, assumes a ready position, and awaits the next ball. When all players have fielded balls to the third-base side, aim the pitching machine to throw balls 20 to 30 feet to the second-base side of the cone. Play continues in the same fashion.

Slight adjustments in the speed of the pitching machine can alter the level of difficulty, but just as in Crossover, the object is to work on footwork, not diving. The machine should never be set so fast that the players have to dive for the ball.

If coaches are skillful with a fungo, live fungo hitting can be used instead of the pitching machine. In many ways, this method is preferable because players get to react to seeing the ball coming off the bat.

First basemen also get valuable work handling throws from the infielders. This game can be scored individually or as a team.

Coaching Points

- Hit balls hard enough so that players don't have time to circle the ball.
- Make sure that players take direct routes to the ground balls.
- Don't let players backhand or forehand the ball if they can get in good fielding position and still make the play.

Follow the Bouncing Ball

2.6

Age: *All*   Skill Level:

Introduction

Young infielders often have problems fielding ground balls because they don't read the ball correctly. Reading the ball is a difficult skill to master and involves being able to judge the speed of the ball, the type of bounce that the ball will have when it reaches the fielder, and the point at which the fielder should break down into fielding position to receive the ball. This game, which I learned from Perry Husband of GuessWorks in California, gives fielders practice reading the ball in stages, which, in turn, helps them learn to coordinate their feet and gloves more proficiently. The use of a softer, bouncier ball allows this game to be played without a fungo bat in a more forgiving environment. This game is also an excellent activity to do indoors on rainy days.

Equipment

Diamond yellow FlexiBall (or similar ball), gloves

Setup

- Players pair up about 70 feet (20 m) apart on the infield or outfield surface. One fields, and the other tosses.
- The player who acts as the feeder should have two FlexiBalls.
- Fielders should be spaced so that they do not interfere with other fielders.

Procedure

Pair players according to ability or position; one player is the fielder, and the other is the feeder. When the fielder assumes the ready position, the feeder should lob toss the ball toward the fielder. Because the balls being used bounce much more than a regular baseball, lobbing them gives the fielders time to adjust. With practice, players should be able to throw the ball with the correct velocity and arc so that the bounces will be challenging yet fair for the fielder to handle.

The feeder can throw the ball directly at the fielder or toward the backhand or forehand side. simulating live ground balls. Caution the feeders not to throw so far to the left or right of the fielder that fielding the ball becomes impossible.

In the first stage of the game, instruct the fielders to read the trajectory and catch the ball on the first bounce and on the short hop in good fielding position.

After they field the ball several times this way, instruct the fielders to field the ball after the second bounce. Now the fielders may have to wait longer or adjust their approach to the ball to be able to reach it on the short hop.

Next, the fielders should try to catch the ball on the third bounce. This skill is more difficult because the bounces with the FlexiBall become shorter in length and quicker as the ball bounces more. The fielders will have to adjust more quickly and break down as they would during a game. As the fielders move through the various steps of this game, provided they play it enough, their coordination should improve tremendously.

The game can continue up to four or five bounces depending on the desires of the coach. The more bounces the ball takes, the more difficult the game becomes. The coach should decide how many tosses, three to five, should be made in each stage. Coaches can devise a simple scoring system to make the game challenging for their infielders.

Coaching Points

- Watch that players field the ball on the short hop—just before or just after it bounces.
- Watch that they break down into good fielding position early in the process.
- Don't let them catch the ball at chest height (which is easy early in the game).
- Make sure that their weight is forward on the balls of their feet.

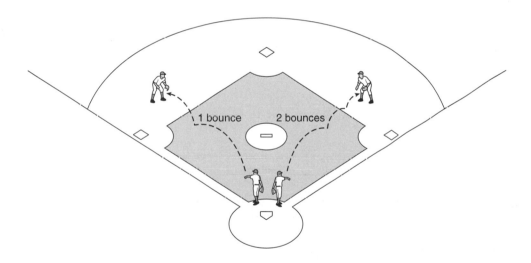

Get 50!

Age: *10 and older*   **Skill Level:**

Introduction

This simple game can be a good way to end practice. It challenges players to focus on their fielding technique and, as the game nears the end, puts pressure on them to perform. The game also emphasizes accurate, not hard, throwing. Because only one fielder at a time is active, the coach can observe each player's footwork in approaching the ball and see where, if anywhere, the fielding technique breaks down. The game is well suited to bad-weather days when practice is moved inside. In fact, because baseballs do not take bad hops on gym floors, the indoor game may be a more accurate indicator of a player's approach to fielding.

Equipment

Baseballs, gloves, fungo bat

Setup

- Players form a single line at the shortstop position or in a corner of the gymnasium.
- The coach stands at home plate or in the opposite corner of the gymnasium with a fungo bat.
- A catcher or other player shags balls for the coach at home.

Procedure

The first person in line breaks off from the group about 15 feet (5 m) and assumes a ready position. The coach or fungo hitter hits a normal ground ball to the fielder. The player executes proper fielding footwork—right, left, field; right, left, throw (for a right-handed player)—and returns the ball to the shagger for the coach or fungo hitter. After fielding, the player goes to the end of the line, and the next player steps out to field the next ball. Continue this process for 50 ground balls. If any player makes an error, either fielding or throwing, the count goes back to zero!

With younger players, reduce the total to 25 or 30. If enough players are present, use two lines and two fungo hitters and have the lines compete against each other. One line could be outfielders and the other infielders. Outfielders could work on their blocking technique or the do-or-die play. The coach should vary the direction and the intensity of the ground balls.

The pressure on players to perform becomes intense, replicating the pressure in a game. Invariably, players will make mistakes, but they are learning to respond to the pressure to perform.

Coaching Points

○ Closely watch fielding and throwing footwork and correct when necessary.

○ The coach should also make sure to stretch and warm up properly before hitting 150 fungoes!

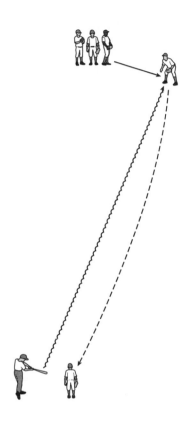

2.8 Get There!

Age: *All*   Skill Level: *All*

Introduction

Someone once said of Hall of Fame shortstop Ozzie Smith, "He plays like he's on a minitrampoline or wearing helium kangaroo shorts." Called the Wizard of Ahhs by many—because that was the usual fan reaction to one of his dazzling fielding gems—Smith was commonly regarded as a model of the perfect shortstop. One trait that separated Smith from the rest of the best was his incredible range, that illusive, hard-to-quantify measurement of how good an infielder is. Basically, range describes how far and how quickly a player can go to his left or right. Although range is hard to measure, most coaches know what it is when they see it, and they want middle infielders, especially, to have extended range. This game helps players extend their range by challenging them to push their limits, react more quickly to the batted ball, and work on getting quicker starts with their feet.

Equipment

Cones, baseballs

Setup

- Place two cones 15 to 20 feet (5 to 6 m) apart on the infield dirt according to the ability and age of players involved.
- The feeder needs five baseballs.

Procedure

One fielder should be positioned midway between the two cones, standing in ready position. A feeder should stand facing the fielder about 15 feet (5 m) away and have five baseballs in his glove or at his feet. The feeder throws ground balls to the fielder randomly to the fielder's left or right between the two cones. The object of the game is for the feeder to get the ball past the fielder or for the fielder to get to the ball and make the fielding play. Points can be given to the fielder or to the feeder according to a system that the coach thinks is appropriate. Players switch sides after five throws. Play may continue for several rounds. If the feeder throws a ball outside the area delineated by the cones, he has points deducted.

The feeder must throw the ball underhanded to keep the game fair. After fielding each ball, the fielder must have time to return to the center of the cone area and assume the ready position before the feeder can throw the next ball. Feeders should vary the direction to which they throw the ball. The ball must bounce at least one time before it reaches the cone area.

The game can be made more difficult by increasing the distance between the cones, by allowing the feeder to throw overhand from farther away, or by incorporating the use of a fungo bat to hit the ground balls.

Coaching Points

- Watch for proper footwork by the fielders, especially the crossover step.
- Watch for proper backhand and forehand technique with the glove hand.

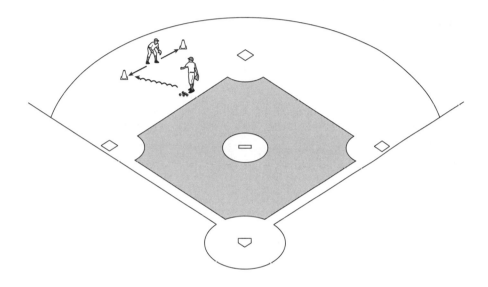

The Hot Box

Age: *All*   **Skill Level:** *All*

Introduction

This game is a more difficult variation of Get There! (page 44). It increases the area the fielder has to cover and further challenges him to stretch the limits of his range. It is similar to the outfield game Five Alive (page 70).

Equipment

Cones, baseballs, fungo bat (optional)

Setup

- Place four cones in a rectangle on the infield, which can vary in size according to the age and skill of the players. The maximum size should be 20 feet by 30 feet by (6 by 9 m).
- The feeder needs six baseballs.

Procedure

The fielder assumes ready position in the center of the rectangle. The feeder, stationed just outside the area of the cones, faces the fielder. The feeder throws five ground balls at various speeds to the fielder. The fielder returns to the center of the rectangle after each ground ball. After throwing five ground balls, the feeder immediately throws a soft popup or looping ball to any spot within the rectangle.

As in Get There! the feeder must throw underhanded. Feeders can vary the direction to which they throw the ball. The ball must bounce at least once before it passes the fielder. This game can be made more difficult by increasing the distance between the cones, by allowing the feeder to throw overhand from farther away, or by incorporating a fungo bat to hit the ground balls.

By increasing the area that the fielder must work, the fielder may have to move both forward and backward diagonally from his ready position, further challenging his range.

Coaching Points

- Watch that players are taking good routes to the ground balls.
- This game may present an opportunity to point out that backhanding the ball is sometimes better than trying to get in front of it.

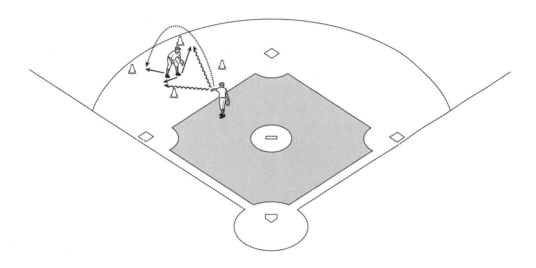

2.10 — Goalie

Age: *All*   **Skill Level:** ⚾⚾

Introduction

Quick hands and reactions are essential fielding skills for all infielders. This game provides opportunities for a fielder to move his feet and hands quickly while in the breakdown fielding position, simulating game conditions. The game has two players challenging each other in 30-second bursts. Ideally, players who are competing for the same position should compete head to head in this game. This game should be played daily as part of an infielder's practice ritual.

Equipment

Several baseballs, cones (or other markers), gloves

Setup

- Place cones or markers 8 feet (2.5 m) apart on the infield dirt, grass, or gym floor. These cones mark the edges of the goal.
- Players partner up, standing 15 feet (5 m) apart and facing each other.
- One player is the fielder and takes a position in the center of the cones.
- The other player is the feeder and stands ready with a ball in his glove and three or four balls on the ground next to him.

Procedure

The feeder throws ground balls to the left, right, and directly at the fielder attempting to get the ball past him. The feeder can throw underhand, backhand, or overhand toward his partner. Thrown balls must hit the ground between the markers at some point before they reach the fielder. The ball should be thrown below knee level of the fielder and hard enough to make it past him. After fielding the ball, the fielder tosses it back underhand to the feeder and returns to his starting position between the cones to await the next toss. If the ball gets through the goal, the feeder takes another ball from his pile and resumes the game with the new ball. After 10 ground balls, players switch positions. They repeat two or three times trying to simulate all types of ground balls.

Scoring: The feeder receives two points for each ball that gets by the fielder, and the fielder receives one point for each caught ball. Balls must be fielded cleanly to earn points. If balls are thrown outside the goal area, the fielder receives a point. The player with the higher total after two or three rounds is the winner.

Variations: (1) Players play the same game but the feeder can add line-drive throws. After the fielder stops the ball, he must return to the center of his area before the feeder throws another ball. (2) The feeder moves back to a spot 25 feet (8 m) from the fielder and uses a bat to hit fungoes to the goal area. The rules in the original game apply, that is, the ball must hit the ground before it passes the fielder.

Coaching Points

- Players should begin in good fielding position—feet shoulder-width apart, knees bent, hands out in front of the body, eyes forward, and buttocks down.
- Make sure that the fielders have a chance to get set again before the feeders throw the next toss.
- For enhancement, widen the area between the cones or shorten the distance between the two players.

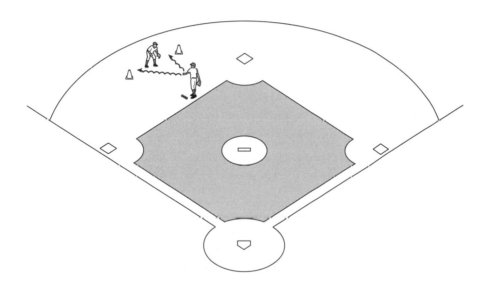

Hold and Go

Age: *12 and older*   **Skill Level:** 🔵🔵🔵🔵

Introduction

The old-school method of choosing first basemen—put players at first who are too big or slow to play anywhere else—no longer applies. First basemen need to be agile and possess catlike reactions. With a runner on first, they have to be able to convert from holding a runner on base to becoming a fielder in the time it takes for a pitch to be delivered. This game challenges first basemen to get into a fielding position that enables them to go left or right quickly to field hard-hit balls on the first-base side. The game also helps them make tactical decisions about whether to throw to second base or simply make an out at first.

Equipment

Baseballs, fungo bat, gloves

Setup

- First basemen line up near first base.
- A middle infielder stations himself on second base.
- The coach stands at home plate with a fungo bat.
- A catcher or other player shags balls for the coach at home.

Procedure

The first player in line gets into position as if he were holding a runner on first base. When the coach or fungo hitter tosses the ball in the air to hit it, the first baseman should move into ready fielding position. The coach then hits hard ground balls to the left or right of the fielder. The fielder must react to the ball, field it or knock it down, and then make the appropriate play. If he fields the ball cleanly, depending on the side to which it was hit and his proximity to first base, he should either throw to second base or step on the bag and then throw to second. If he knocks the ball down, he must scramble to the ball and then make a decision about what to do.

   If the ball gets past or through the fielder, the next person in line takes his place and the original fielder moves to the end of the line. The coach tosses another ball, and play continues as long as deemed necessary. When using a catcher as a shagger, as an added twist, the coach, instead of hitting the tossed ball with his fungo, can catch the ball and flip it to the catcher, who then makes a pickoff throw to first base. This option forces the first baseman to work on returning to the bag and making tags on pickoff plays.

   Points can be awarded for the number of balls each player fields or knocks down. Points can be deducted if the coach thinks that the player made an error in judgment.

Coaching Points

● This game creates an opportunity for coaches to show first basemen how to stand when holding on runners.

● Coaches should work on the first basemen's footwork so that they get into ready position comfortably. Some feel better hopping off the base, whereas others take a crossover step and glide into position.

● Players must get into a bent-knee, athletic position quickly.

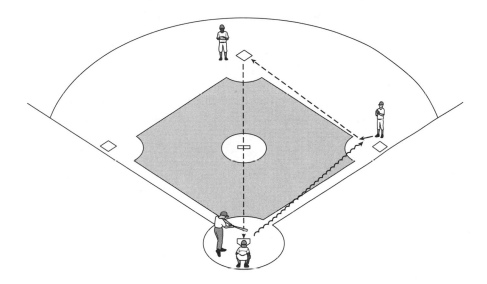

Hot-Corner Reaction

Age: *High school and older*   **Skill Level:** ⚾⚾⚾⚾

Introduction

Third base has long been called the hot corner because of its proximity to home plate and because third basemen often play in front of the bag to cut off the possibility of a drag bunt. Sharply hit balls quickly reach the fielder, who often doesn't have time to do much except get his glove up to try to field the ball before it hits him. Hall of Fame pitcher turned announcer Dizzy Dean once said of a great third baseman, "He'd have played a lot longer except his chest gave out on him!" Such is the plight of the third baseman—react or be hit. The objective of this game is to heighten the awareness and reactions of third basemen so that they are able to get at least a glove on the ball. When played regularly, it can quicken the hands of even the slowest reacting fielders.

Equipment

Bucket of tennis balls, rag balls, Wiffle balls, or baseballs; gym mat; fielder's gloves

Setup

- Third basemen pair up.
- Place a gym mat on the floor if playing the game indoors.

Procedure

Fielders pair off and face each other 10 to 12 feet (3 to 3.5 m) apart. One player kneels on both knees with his glove hand and throwing hand out in front of his body as if he is in fielding position. The other player takes a ball from a bucket and underhands it with some zest toward his kneeling partner. The fielder tries to field the ball with his glove. Immediately after catching the ball, the fielder tosses it to either side and prepares for another thrown ball. After the feeder tosses the first ball, he immediately grabs another ball from the bucket and tosses it in the same fashion. The game works best when feeders toss the ball to many locations—at the shoulders, at the knees, at the waist, at the face, above the head, 1 foot (30 cm) outside the glove side of the kneeling player, 1 foot outside the throwing side, and so on. The feeder must not throw too far away from the kneeling fielder. The kneeling fielder must maintain his balance. After 10 tosses, players switch positions and continue play. Three or four rounds or five minutes should be sufficient.

If the fielder catches the ball or knocks it down with his glove so that it stays in front of him, the fielder gets a point. Knocking the ball down is sometimes all that a third baseman can do on a play anyway. A toss too far to one side also counts as a point for the fielder. The tosser should make the game as difficult as possible to challenge his partner. Keep a daily score and post results.

Coaching Points

- Make certain that players get their gloves into the proper position.
- Players should have their fingers up for balls above the waist and fingers down for balls below the waist.

Hot Shots

Age: *12 and older* **Skill Level:** 🟤🟤🟤🟤

Introduction

Quaint little phrases can be great memory aids both in the classroom and on the athletic field. Anyone who has ever had a music class in elementary school learned the phrase "Every good boy does fine" to help remember the notes on the main lines of the treble clef. First basemen must often make a split-second judgment about balls hit to their right. Do they try to field them and let the pitcher or second baseman cover the base, or do they let the ball go and let the second baseman field it? This game is based on a mnemonic device that provides a useful rule for first basemen: If it's hot, give it a shot; if it's slow, let it go! The game provides enough repetitions that the first baseman's decision about whether or not to field becomes automatic. If a ball is hit hard to the right of the first baseman, chances are that the second baseman will not have a chance to reach it, so the first baseman must learn to make an effort to field this kind of ball. If a ball is hit slowly in that direction, the second baseman will normally be able to get to the ball and make the play.

Equipment

Baseballs, fungo bat, gloves

Setup

- First basemen line up near first base.
- Second basemen assume normal depth in the infield.
- The coach stands at home plate with a fungo bat.
- A catcher or other player shags balls for the coach at home.

Procedure

The first player in line takes his normal position on the diamond without a runner on base. The coach hits a ground ball or line drive to the right side of the player. Depending on the speed and location of the ball, the first baseman either attempts to field it or allows it to go by and runs to cover first base. After each fungo, the player goes to the end of the line and the next player takes his place.

Coaches need to vary the location or speed with which they hit the ball. They should randomly hit slow, medium, and hard-hit balls. Occasionally, they can hit a line drive or two, again varying the speed.

Coaches can award points to players based on judgment and fielding skill.

Coaching Point

○ Challenge players to discover their range by hitting progressively harder balls to their right.

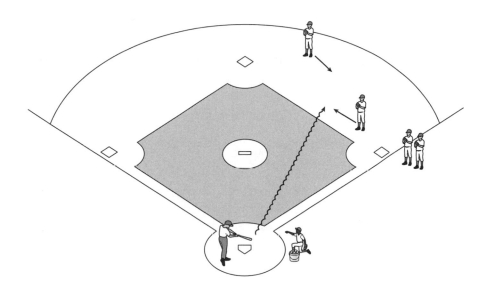

Mass Fungo

Age: *12 and older*   **Skill Level:**

Introduction

Making sure that players get enough daily fielding repetitions is a constant concern of coaches. Daily one-on-one drills can fill some of the gap, but nothing makes up for fielding balls live off a bat. This infield warm-up game uses the entire squad and gives every infielder numerous fielding reps in a short amount of time. Used as a pregame warm-up, the game gives infielders an opportunity to get to know the feel of an infield quickly, which is especially important at an unfamiliar park.

Equipment

Fungo bats, baseballs

Setup

- Infielders assume their positions on the field.
- Four fungo hitters assume positions directly opposite each infield position.
- A shagger stands to the right of each fungo hitter.
- At least four baseballs should be placed at each fungo station.

Procedure

Infielders should occupy a position on the infield dirt on the outfield side of the baseline nearest them. Fungo hitters should stand in foul territory directly opposite the fielders to whom they will be hitting. For example, the fungo hitter who is hitting to the first basemen should be positioned outside the third-base line and to the left of home plate. The fungo hitter hitting to the second basemen is also stationed outside the third-base line but just to the right of third base. The fungo hitters along the first-base line who are hitting to the shortstops and third basemen are stationed similarly outside the first-base line.

Fielders assume their ready positions, and fungo hitters begin hitting ground balls to the fielders opposite them (that is, the fungo hitter for the first basemen hits ground balls only to the first basemen). After fielding the ball, the infielder tosses the ball back to the shagger for his fungo hitter and again assumes his ready position. If there is more than one fielder at a position, fielders should take turns fielding balls from the fungo hitter.

If a ball gets by the fielder, instead of chasing it, he should again assume his ready position and wait for another ball to be hit to him. After he tosses it back to the shagger, the fielder can then retrieve the missed ball. Coaches should predetermine how many balls each fielder should receive; each fielder can easily get 25 balls or more in a 15-minute period.

A tally should be kept of how many balls each fielder fielded cleanly. This count can heighten the competition among fielders at the same position and gives the coach a chance to evaluate players.

Outfielders and catchers can serve as fungo hitters and shaggers. All baseball players should learn to hit fungoes anyway because doing so helps improve bat control.

Balls should be hit left and right of fielders at varying speeds—some hard shots, some normal ground balls, and some soft rollers. A word of caution is necessary here. Fungo hitters should not hit at the same time and should always be aware of what the fielder nearest them is doing. For example, the fungo hitter who is hitting to the second basemen should never hit a ball if the third baseman is charging in on a slowly hit ball from his fungo hitter. The fungo hitter nearest first base should observe the same precaution.

Coaching Points

- Coaches should circulate during the game and provide individual instruction.
- They should ask infielders to lob the ball back to the shagger. Because they will be making many throws, throwing hard across the infield would strain their arms.

PFP
(With a Twist)

Age: *High school and older* **Skill Level:** 🏐🏐🏐🏐

Introduction

A sure sign that spring is just around the corner is film footage on the nightly sports show from spring training of pitchers taking fielding practice. Pitchers simulate pitches and then automatically run toward first base to cover the bag as the first baseman fields a fungo and tosses it to the pitcher. This drill has become a staple of the baseball regimen—but it's a useless drill unless some gamelike aspects are incorporated. PFP (With a Twist) is a game designed to add real-time, gamelike features to the typical PFP drill by forcing players to read situations and make appropriate responses.

Equipment

Fungo bat, bucket of baseballs

Setup

- ◉ Pitchers stand in a line between the mound and second base. One pitcher assumes a position on the rubber with a ball in his glove.
- ◉ A catcher in full gear is in receiving position behind home plate.
- ◉ Infielders are stationed at all infield positions.
- ◉ Players waiting to serve as base runners are in foul territory near first base and home plate.
- ◉ A coach with a fungo bat is in the batter's box at home plate.

Procedure

A runner takes a primary lead off first base. The first pitcher throws a pitch to the catcher. After the pitcher throws the ball, the coach hits a fungo somewhere on the right side of the infield. When the ball is hit, another runner, who is stationed even with home plate in foul territory outside the lefthander's batter's box, runs to first base. Fielders react to the ball and the runners. The coach should mix up where the ball is hit to simulate game conditions. Coaches can hit balls to the first baseman or the pitchers or between them. Pitchers have to make split-second decisions and react accordingly. If more than one catcher is available, catchers should rotate after each play. After the play, the next pitcher takes the rubber and play continues.

Coaches can roll the ball out in front of the plate to simulate bunts or occasionally hit the ball slightly to the right of the pitcher to keep the pitchers honest. Otherwise, they would automatically move toward first base.

The game can be made more difficult by placing runners at first and second or only at second base. This scenario forces a different level of decision making on the infielders. Pitchers then have to react not only to the runner from home but also to runners on the bases and make throws accordingly. With runners on the bases, other fielders also become involved in the tactical process. For example, an occasional fungo to the first baseman might facilitate the start of a 3-6-1 double play.

Coaching Points

- Make sure that pitchers break to their left side to cover first base on all balls hit to their left.
- Remind catchers to be vocal and let pitchers know where to throw the ball.
- Freeze replay, as discussed in the introduction, works well here because it emphasizes the decision-making process about whether to make a play on the runner at second or third or to take the automatic out at first base.

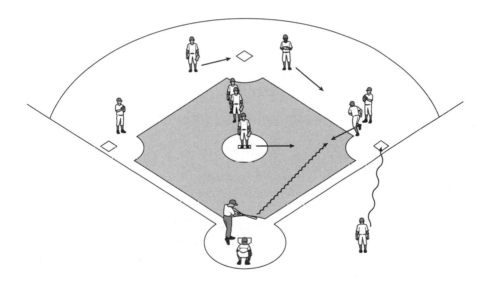

Slow-Roller Throwing

Age: *High school and older*   **Skill Level:** 🔵🔵🔵🔵

Introduction

One of the hardest plays to make in baseball is fielding a slowly rolling ball and making a swift, accurate throw. The key to accomplishing this play is making the throw while on the run. Usually this means throwing with a sidearm motion off the wrong foot. If the fielder tries to stop and get his balance, the runner will usually beat the throw. This two-person game gives players at all infield positions daily practice in the throwing motion without having to worry about the fielding portion of the play.

Equipment

Baseballs, gloves

Setup

- Fielders pair up 15 feet (5 m) apart.
- For safety, pairs should be spaced at least 10 feet (3 m) from the next nearest pair.
- One baseball is on the ground about 1 foot (30 cm) in front of the fielder's left foot.

Procedure

After players have paired up, one player in each pair assumes a backhand fielding position with the glove-side foot forward of the throwing-side foot. The other player acts as the target. The fielder in backhand position places a ball about 1 foot (30 cm) in front of his glove-side foot and slightly to the inside of that foot. After placing the ball the player resumes an erect backhand position. Next, the player bends down to pick up the ball while at the same time lifting his throwing-side leg in the air (see figure). From this awkward balance point, after picking up the ball, the player flip throws the ball to his partner by drawing his elbow back and then slinging the ball under his chest. Partners should give good targets. A thrower receives a point if his partner catches the ball without moving his feet. After five throws, partners switch positions. This game forces infielders to find a good balance point from which they can make strong, accurate throws.

After players have become accomplished in this skill from 15 feet (5 m), the distance between partners should be lengthened to increase the challenge. Coaches can invent other scoring systems to make the game harder or fairer.

Coaching Points

- Watch that players start the throw by bringing the throwing-arm elbow back first.
- Players must keep their weight on the front foot.
- Caution players to maintain their balance when making throws.

Spin and Fire

Age: *12 and older*   **Skill Level:** ⚾⚾⚾⚾⚾

Introduction

This game is the second baseman's version of Backhand Force (page 30). Instead of working on the backhand play, however, this game works with the equivalent tough force play for the second baseman—the forehand play in the hole behind first base. Great second basemen like Orlando Hudson of the Diamondbacks routinely make this play to cut down the lead runner in a force play. Normally, on a ball hit far to a second baseman's left with less than two outs, the fielder automatically makes the easier play at first base for the out, but doing so allows the lead runner to reach scoring position at second. An infielder who can make this difficult force play can save more than a few runs for his team in the course of a season. This game helps him gain confidence with the skill.

Equipment

Gloves, balls, bases, four cones

Setup

- Mark spots with lining chalk on the infield where shortstops and second basemen should stand when at double-play depth.
- Place a shortstop at double-play depth on the infield.
- Second basemen stand in a line at double-play depth.
- Place four cones 3 to 4 feet (1 to 1.2 m) apart at various spots in the infield hole behind first base. Place cones so that cone 1 is closest to the second baseman and cone 4 is farthest away.

Procedure

The first second baseman, with a ball in his glove, assumes his ready position at double-play depth in the infield on the spot marked with chalk. On command of the coach or another player, the second baseman sprints to the first cone, simulates fielding a ball at that spot, pivots to his glove-hand side, planting his right foot firmly as he does so, and turns and throws to the shortstop, who has assumed a pivot position at second base. After the throw, the next second baseman assumes his position at the mark and performs the same routine. After all second basemen have completed the first throw, the game continues with each second baseman sprinting in turn to cones 2, 3, and 4.

By starting with the ball already in the glove, the fielder can concentrate only on getting his body set and making the throw to the base. Placing the cones farther from the fielder or at various locations from the front of the infield to the outfield grass will make the game more challenging. Placing the cones even deeper on the outfield grass presents an exciting challenge for the fielder. As players become adept at making this throw, rearrange the cones to add difficulty. The game can be scored based on the accuracy of the throws and the quickness of the fielder in transferring from fielding to throwing position.

Coaching Points

- Make certain that the second basemen hop on to the throwing-side foot after fielding. This technique helps them stop their momentum and make firm, overhand throws.
- Make sure that they get their feet under their hips and the glove-side shoulder pointed at the target. Not doing this will lead to rushing the throw and throwing across the body, causing the ball to tail away from the target.

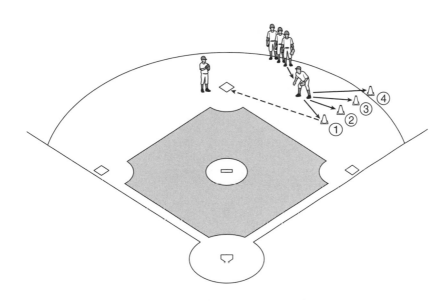

Z Ball Reaction

Age: *High school and older*   Skill Level: ⚾⚾⚾⚾

Introduction

Every Boston Red Sox fan knows all about bad hops—just ask them about the 1986 World Series! Bad hops are part of the game, but if players can improve their glove-hand reactions, the chances of a bad hop being disastrous are greatly reduced. This game keeps players on their toes and helps them react to bad bounces while also increasing their focus and quickness with their feet. At the same time, its unpredictability makes it great fun. The unique shape of the Z ball guarantees that no two bounces will be alike. (Z balls are available from numerous sources.)

Equipment

Z balls or similar devices, gloves, cones

Setup

- Partners pair up 15 to 20 feet (5 to 6 m) apart.
- Place cones about 6 feet (2 m) apart and 6 feet in front of the fielder.

Procedure

Pair players according to ability or position. One player is the fielder, and the other is the feeder. The fielder assumes ready position. The feeder tosses a Z ball toward the fielder, trying to bounce the ball within the confines of the cones. When the feeder tosses the ball, the fielder should move into fielding position according to the direction in which the ball was thrown and field the ball. Feeders can vary the speed of their tosses, which affects the way that the ball bounces and challenges the fielder. Various scoring systems can be used for this game, but the simplest would be to keep track of the number of balls fielded cleanly.

As players become more adept in their handling of the Z ball, increase the distance between the cones by several feet (a meter or so). The fielders will have to cover a larger area, giving them opportunities to work on backhand and forehand bad hops, and the feeder will have more leeway in his tossing area.

Variation: One of the first baseman's most important skills is the ability to field balls thrown in the dirt by infielders while maintaining first-base contact with his foot. Moving the Z Ball Reaction game over to first base helps first basemen sharpen their focusing skills and gives them practice moving their gloves quickly while in the stride position. The feeder should be about 30 feet (10 m) from the first baseman and use the Z ball to imitate a throw in the dirt by an infielder. When the feeder tosses the ball, the first baseman should assume his position on the base and stretch for the ball. This variation allows the first baseman to practice scooping the ball and quickly moving the glove from the glove-down position to the backhand position.

Coaching Points

- With younger players, coaches should do the tossing to lessen the chance of injury.
- Make sure that players keep their weight forward on the balls of the feet when fielding.

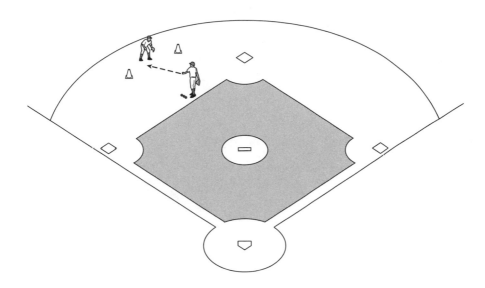

## CHAPTER 3

OUTFIELD GAMES

Two-Line Communication

Age: *All* **Skill Level:** *All*

Introduction

A batter hits a lofting fly ball into the gap between two outfielders. Both fielders sprint to the ball, each intent on making the catch and oblivious to the other's racing advance. Few occurrences in baseball are more frightening than watching two players speed toward each other about to engage in a head-on collision. The chance for injury in this scenario is obviously great. Most of these sorts of disasters can be avoided if players practice communicating often. This game provides practice in both the proper technique for fielding balls in the gaps and communication between outfielders.

Equipment

Pitching machine, fungo bat, baseballs

Setup

- Outfielders form two groups—one in center field and one in left or right field.
- A fungo hitter, coach, or pitching machine is stationed near second base.
- A shagger for return throws stands near the fungo hitter, coach, or pitching machine.

Procedure

The two groups of fielders should be about 100 feet (30 m) apart. Play begins when the coach hits a fly ball somewhere between the two lines of fielders. One fielder from each line moves toward the ball to field it. When one of the fielders calls for the ball, the other fielder should immediately move into position to back up the play. Fielders should loudly call, "Mine, mine, mine" when they have made the decision to field the ball. The fielder who has not made the call for the catch should respond by saying, "Yours, yours, yours." After the catch the outfielders switch lines. The coach then hits another fungo into the same area. Play continues until the coach feels that the outfielders have had sufficient practice in the skill. Scoring, if done, should be done on a team basis with emphasis on good communication.

A pitching machine can be used instead of a fungo, especially when the coach wants to replicate the same sort of fly ball each time.

Ground balls should be mixed in with the fly balls to give additional practice in backing up. With younger players, reduce the distance between the fielding lines and toss the ball in the air by hand until they have learned how to call for a ball and back up. This method lessens the chance of injury.

Coaching Points

● Make certain that players are extremely vocal when calling for the ball. They have to shout!

● Make sure that backup outfielders respond loudly to eliminate the chance for confusion.

● Emphasize a priority system.

● Watch that players do not call for the ball too early; the ball should reach its highest point or be starting downward before a player makes a call.

● Coach the backup outfielder to back up low, especially on balls that are not called for until very late and on balls where a collision is possible.

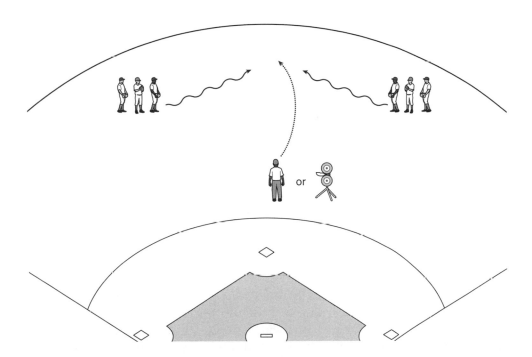

3.2 Five Alive

Age: *12 and older*   **Skill Level:** ⚾⚾⚾

Introduction

In playing this game, outfielders will develop the strategies and tactics needed to catch fly balls, play balls off the wall, and react to game situations. The game will also improve their conditioning. This game should be played as often as necessary, at least several times per week at practice. As outfielders learn to stretch their limits at practice, they increase their confidence and become more adept at recognizing balls that they can attempt to catch during games. As the season progresses, coaches should add additional challenges and variations as necessary.

Equipment

Six baseballs, four cones or other suitable markers

Setup

- Place four cones (markers) in a square approximately 20 feet (6 m) on a side.
- One player is the fielder and assumes position in the middle of the square with his glove on.
- The other player is the feeder and assumes position outside the box formed by the cones and facing player A.

Procedure

Outfielders partner up and work in the outfield. Place four markers around the fielder, creating a square 20 feet (6 m) on a side. The feeder tries to get the ball past the fielder using a looping throw to simulate a fly ball. Each fielder receives six balls per round. When the fielder is about to catch the first ball, the feeder releases the second ball so that it will land, if uncaught, anywhere within the 20-foot square. He does the same with the next three balls. The feeder must throw underhand with an arc, much like a slow-pitch softball pitch. After throwing the fifth ball, the feeder rolls a ground ball into the zone, which the fielder must stop from going through. The players then switch positions. Players perform as many sets as the coach deems necessary. The feeder receives two points for each ball that hits the ground and one point for a ground ball that gets past the fielder. The fielder receives one point for each caught ball and two points for stopping the ground ball.

Coaching Point

● Because this game will rapidly fatigue players, make certain to allow enough rest time after each rotation.

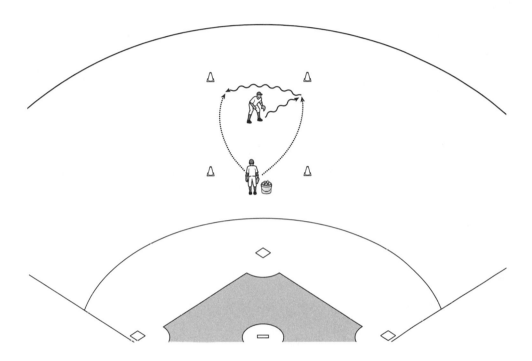

Harvey's Wallbanger

Age: *12 and older*   **Skill Level:** 🔘🔘🔘

Introduction

During the early 1980s the Milwaukee Brewers had a potent lineup of home-run hitters under manager Harvey Kuenn. As a result, the team earned the nickname Harvey's Wallbangers as a play on words about a popular refreshment at the time. Not only balls go crashing off or over walls; outfielders also make their share of contact with solid objects. Young players seldom receive enough opportunities to learn how to make catches near a wall or to play balls on the rebound off a fence. This game gives outfielders a chance to do both. Players learn how to sense their relationship to the fence or wall without taking their eyes off the ball and how to read and react to caroms off the fence.

Equipment

Six baseballs, four cones or other suitable markers

Setup

- Using a fence or wall as the back marker for the area, place four cones in a square approximately 40 feet (12 m) on a side.
- Divide players into groups of three—each group comprises a fielder, feeder, and cutoff player.
- The fielder assumes a ready position near the front of the square facing the infield.
- The feeder stands about 15 feet (5 m) in front of the area, facing player A.
- The cutoff player stands about 100 feet (30 m) from the wall in a line with one of the bases.

Procedure

Players work in groups of three within a 40-foot (12 m) square, created by placing four markers around the fielder. The feeder throws fly balls to the wall within the area bounded by the cones. The fielder must read the arc of the ball and run to the wall to attempt the catch. After making the catch, the fielder throws to the cutoff player and then returns to the front of the square to await another ball. After five fly balls, players rotate. The feeder becomes the fielder, the cutoff player becomes the feeder, and the fielder becomes the cutoff. Players may throw balls underhand or overhand toward the wall as long as they remain within the marked area.

The fielder should keep his eyes on the ball as he retreats to make the catch. On balls close to the wall, he should sense that he is approaching the wall by feeling the warning track and by using his throwing hand to find the wall. The feeder may throw line drives over the fielder's head that bounce off the wall. When this happens, the fielder should pull up, play the ball off the wall, and then make a strong throw to the cutoff player. At least one ball in each round should imitate a line drive off the wall.

The fielder receives one point for each fly ball caught and another point for each accurate throw. If the cutoff must move considerably, no points are awarded. Deduct a point if a ball caroms off the wall and gets past the fielder. Coaches may decide to award more points for difficult catches, such as leaping or climbing catches over the wall. If the feeder throws the ball out of the park, deduct points from the feeder's total.

Coaching Point

◉ Make sure that players watch the ball and not the fence. Outfielders fail to catch many catchable balls near a wall because they peek at the wall and lose sight of the ball.

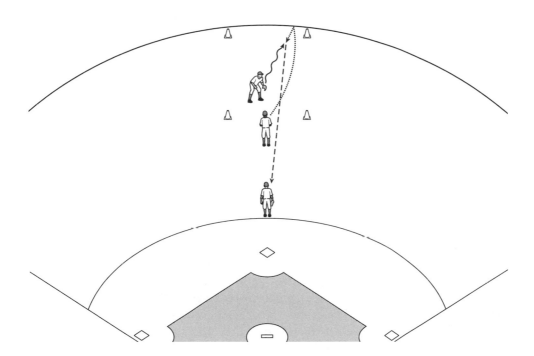

3.4 — **Hustle!** —

Age: *10 and older*   **Skill Level:** 🟤🟤

Introduction

The comic strip *Peanuts* has done a great disservice to baseball! As much as I enjoy reading the strip, the image of Charlie Brown, the lonely right fielder, has forever maligned outfielders. Many coaches still don't spend enough time working with their outfielders, instead concentrating practice time on infield and pitching. But consider this: The outfielders are a team's last line of defense. Outfielders have to be prepared and focused at all times. No outfielder, unlike poor ol' Charlie, has the luxury of picking dandelions in the middle of a game. One of the qualities that outfielders need is stamina. This game works outfielders hard while giving them practice in game situations. Thanks goes to Tom McLamore, coach at Farmington High School in New Mexico, for the inspiration for this game.

Equipment

Fungo bat, bucket of balls

Setup

- ◎ All outfielders form a line along one of the foul lines.
- ◎ A coach with fungo bat stands in the infield at second base.
- ◎ An infielder or catcher serves as a feeder for the coach.

Procedure

All outfielders line up on the left-field foul line. On command, the first fielder begins running across the outfield toward the right-field foul line in an arc, following the arc of the fence. The second fielder gives the first fielder a 40-foot (12 m) head start and then begins running in the same direction. A coach stands in the infield dirt near second base with a bucket of balls and a feeder–shagger and hits fungoes to the first fielder, trying to lead the fielder as a quarterback in football would lead a receiver. The fielder catches the ball, immediately drops it behind him, and continues to run. The second fielder retrieves the ball, puts it in his glove, and continues to follow. The coach continues to hit challenging line drives, fly balls, and ground balls at the fielder until the fielder reaches the right-field foul line. The coach then commands the next outfielder waiting at the left-field foul line to start running and continues to hit balls. When all outfielders reach the right-field line, they return in the opposite direction as the coach fungoes more balls. On the return run, the original fielder becomes the retriever and vice versa.

Outfielders can score points for every ball they field cleanly. Keep a record and post the results. This game should be played at least once a week, and it can be fit in while other position players are working on their skills on other parts of the field.

Coaches should be certain to hit fungoes that make outfielders stretch the limits of their athletic ability but are not too difficult or unfair.

Coaching Points

- Give enough rest between rounds because of the strenuous nature of the game.
- Make certain that outfielders are running on the balls of their feet. As they fatigue, they might start running on their heels.

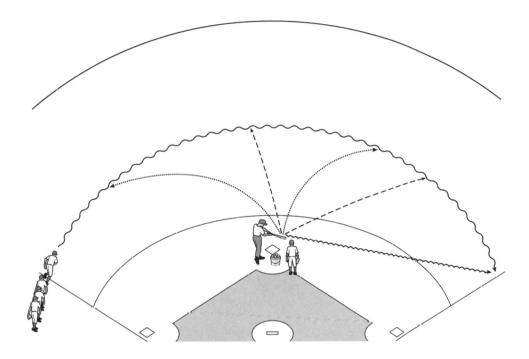

3.5 — Do or Die

Age: *12 and older*   **Skill Level:** 🥎🥎🥎🥎

Introduction

A skill that all outfielders need to master, especially at upper levels, is the do-or-die play—being able to field the ball on the run and make a quick throw to a base. This type of play has inherent risks because outfield turf does not always allow true bounces of the ball, but outfielders still need to work on the play to be able to cut down runners who are trying to advance. This game gives fielders practice in the footwork necessary for the play, yet it does not call for long throws that would tax players' arms. The game also calls for accuracy.

Equipment

Balls, archery target on a stand, netting or backstop fencing

Setup

- Have outfielders line up at the edge of the outfield about 100 feet (30 m) from and facing an outfield fence or similar fencing.
- A fungo hitter or coach stands near the fence with a bucket of balls. (A pitching machine could substitute for a fungo hitter.)
- Place an archery target simulating a cutoff or relay person near the outfield fence. If an archery target is unavailable, a similar target could be taped to the fence.

Procedure

The coach or fungo hitter hits bouncing ball to the first outfielder in line. The outfielder should take the proper approach to the ball, field it, transfer it to his throwing hand, and make a throw toward the target. After the first player has fielded the ball and thrown, he returns to the end of the line, the next player assumes a ready position, and the coach hits another ground ball. Points can be given to fielders for coming close to hitting the target or for hitting a particular part of the target. For example, hitting the top left quadrant of the target might be worth five points, hitting anywhere else on the top half of the target could be worth three points, a near miss could be worth two points, and so on. Coaches could even put the outline of a cutoff player on the target to simulate reality more closely. The important thing is that the target be about the height of a player standing in cutoff position. Using a target instead of a player gives players immediate visual feedback and allows infielders to work on infield skills on another part of the field. Also, by reducing the distance, outfielders do not have to throw as far and will not fatigue their arms.

If coaches want fielders to throw longer distances, they could set the target at a point where the throws from the outfielders would take one bounce before hitting the target. The height of the target should be adjusted accordingly.

Coaching Point

● This game provides an excellent opportunity for coaches to emphasize good crow-hop technique. Watch to make sure that players field the ball outside their glove-side leg and time the scoop of the ball to coincide with the landing of the glove-side foot.

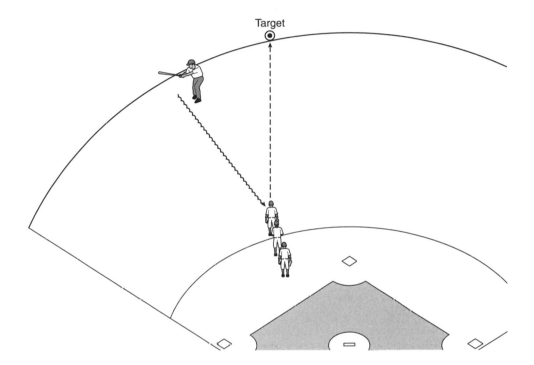

3.6

Cut 'Em Down

Age: *12 and older*   **Skill Level:** ⚾⚾⚾⚾

Introduction

Few plays in baseball are more exciting than watching an outfielder cut down a lead runner at third base or home plate. This game gives fielders an opportunity to work on their long throws in real-time, gamelike situations. It also allows base runners to work on their baserunning skills and infielders a chance to make quality relays.

Equipment

Fungo hitter, bucket of baseballs

Setup

- Outfielders take positions in left, center, and right fields.
- A fielder is at third base and a shortstop is in cutoff position.
- A fungo hitter, coach, or pitching machine is stationed on the infield grass.
- A line of runners wearing helmets is at first base or second base.
- A coach is in the third-base coaching box.

Procedure

Fielders assume their ready positions. The first runner in line at first base takes a 12-foot (3.5 m) lead. Play begins when the coach signals the runner to take a secondary lead at the base. and then hits a ground ball to one of the outfielders. The runner breaks on the sound of the ball hitting the bat and attempts to go to third on the play, depending on where the ball is hit. If the ball is hit in front of him, to left field or left-center field, the runner must judge whether he should advance. If the ball is hit behind him, the runner must pick up the signal to advance from the third-base coach.

The outfielders must come up throwing to third base to try to cut down the runner. The shortstop must get into good cut–relay position and execute good technique. Runners are not allowed to slide into the base. If the ball beats the runner to the base, he is out. Award two points for every outfield throw that beats a runner and one point for every runner who beats the throw. Coaches can vary the scoring to promote aggressiveness on the bases.

The fungo hitter should hit the ground balls at various speeds, hitting some softly to left field to challenge the runners. Balls should be hit left and right of the fielders to create as many variables as possible.

A variation of the game is to start the runners at second base and have the outfielders throw home.

Both games provide opportunities for coaches to enhance their judgments about when to send a runner and when to hold him.

Coaching Points

- Encourage players to make their own baserunning decisions when the ball is hit in front of them.
- Have players consider the arm strength of the outfielder, which arm the outfielder throws with, how hard the ball was hit, the direction of the ball, and the field conditions.
- Direct players to make their decision to go or not go when their foot hits second base.

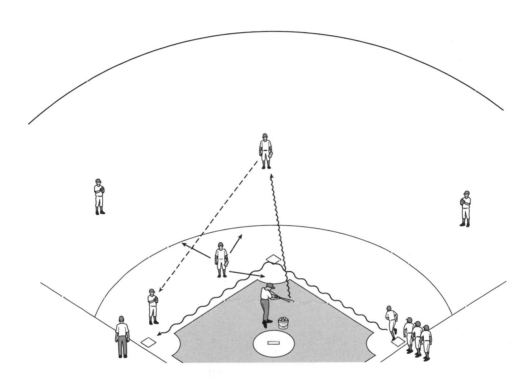

Line Drive

Age: *12 and older*   **Skill Level:** ⚾⚾⚾⚾

Introduction

The most difficult balls to catch are sometimes the ones hit directly at fielders, especially line drives hit straight to an outfielder. The ball may not only be rising or sinking but also moving to the left or right of the fielder, depending on whether the batter is left-handed or right-handed. This game gives outfielders opportunities to hone their skills on line drives and become more adept at reading what a ball might do.

Equipment

Regular pitching machine or ATEC Hitting Streak, baseballs, cone

Setup

- Place a pitching machine at the edge of the infield dirt or along one of the foul lines, depending on power source.
- Place a cone in the outfield as a starting point for outfielders in a direct line with the pitching machine about 150 feet (45 m) away.
- Assemble outfielders in a line near the cone.
- Have a bucket of balls on hand near the machine.
- A shagger should be stationed near the machine to retrieve return throws from the outfielders.
- A coach or player serves as feeder for the machine.

Procedure

The pitching machine should be preset to shoot line drives in the direction of the cone. Set the speed control of the machine so that balls hit the ground about 15 to 20 feet (5 to 8 m) in front of the cone. The game begins with an outfielder in ready position near the cone. When the coach or player drops a ball into the pitching machine, the outfielder should take a hard drop step back and then sprint in to catch the ball. After catching the ball, the outfielder throws the ball back toward the infield shagger and then runs to the end of the outfield line. Another outfielder steps forward and assumes his ready position on the field, and the feeder inserts another ball. Play continues for as long as the coach chooses.

Skillful manipulation of the speed settings on the pitching machine can make the ball fly various distances before it lands. By adjusting the speed, feeders can force outfielders to run in faster or slower for balls or even create circumstances in which the outfielder has to make a diving catch. By nudging the legs of the machine a bit, feeders can also make the balls fly left or right of the cone, giving fielders even more area to cover. When fielders have had sufficient practice coming in on line drives, the feeder can increase the speed of the machine to simulate line drives over the heads of outfielders to give them work on running back on deep line drives.

Outfielders can compete against each other, and points can be awarded for correctly judging the flight path of a ball and getting to the right location on time.

Coaching Points

- Make certain that outfielders catch line drives with the fingers of their glove pointed up for balls above the waist and down for balls below the waist.
- Shoot balls to both the right and the left of the fielder to simulate game situations more accurately.

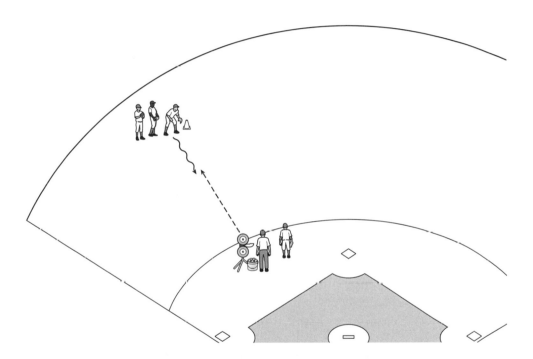

3.8 — **Fence**

Introduction

Ken Griffey Jr., one of the finest outfielders of all time, has made a career out of game-saving, leaping grabs at the outfield wall—often with little regard for his personal safety. Making this sort of play is every outfielder's fantasy. But the reality is that the play is difficult to make unless practiced. At least once or twice during the course of a season, outfielders should practice making catches at the fence or jumping at the fence in an attempt to stop a home run.

Equipment

Baseballs, outfield fence, cones, pitching machine (optional)

Setup

- Outfielders pair up near the fence. One outfielder will be a feeder, the other a fielder.
- Place cones to mark a 40-foot square area near the fence.
- Optional: Set up pitching machine at edge of infield aimed toward the outfield fence.

Procedure

One outfielder acting as fielder assumes a ready position facing the infield and at the forward part of the area marked by the cones. The other outfielder, the feeder, faces the fielder. The feeder throws high-looping fly balls toward the fence. As soon as a ball is thrown, the fielder should execute a drop step and attempt to field the fly ball. Feeders should throw the balls in an arc so that they either hit off the top of the fence or land very near the fence. After five or six throws, outfielders should change positions. As an option, a pitching machine can be set to throw high-lofting fly balls close to the fence. A coach should be used as a feeder for the machine as a safety precaution. When the coach drops a ball into the machine, the outfielder should read the arc of the ball and sprint to the fence in an attempt to catch it. With skill and minute adjustments to the speed of the machine, the balls can just barely clear the fence, giving outfielders practice in making leaping catches. Not all balls need be thrown against the fence.

Caution: Make sure that the outfield fence is protected with covering.

Coaching Points

● Teach players to watch the flight of the ball and not peek at the fence. They should use their throwing hands to find the fence while keeping their eyes on the ball.

● Make sure players time their leaps so that they don't jump too early.

● Remind players of the depth of the warning track and to use the feel of the feet on the track to guide their distance from the wall.

● Encourage players to get to the wall early and not drift slowly. It is always much easier to come in toward the infield than it is to go back to make a catch.

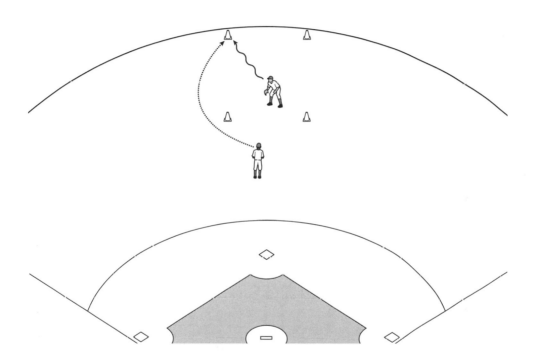

Turn and Burn

Age: *12 and older*   **Skill Level:** 🔘🔘🔘🔘

Introduction

In an instructional book, Hall of Famer Joe DiMaggio, one of the greatest center fielders of all time, advised young players, "No outfielder is a real workman unless he can turn his back on the ball, run his legs off, and take the catch over his shoulder. Backpedaling outfielders get nowhere." One of the worst mistakes an outfielder can make is to backpedal, as DiMaggio said, or to drift to a fly ball, to run lazily after a ball that looks as though it will be easy to catch. Coaches can probably attribute many of their gray hairs to watching outfielders drift to balls only to see them sail over the fielders' heads at the last second, badly misjudged. This game addresses one of the fundamentals of outfield play—going back hard on the first few steps on any batted ball. It gives outfielders practice turning away from a ball and sprinting to a spot where they think it will land, and it helps them sharpen their judgment regarding ball trajectory and speed.

Equipment

Pitching machine, baseballs, cones

Setup

- Place two cones in a line about 40 feet (12 m) apart and 100 feet (30 m) from second base.
- Set up a pitching machine to one side of second base, aimed toward the outfield.
- Mark an X with lining chalk in center field as a starting point for outfielders. The X should be about 30 feet (10 m) from the cones between the cones and second base.
- Place a bucket of balls at the machine.
- A shagger should cover second base to retrieve throws from the outfield.
- Outfielders form a line near the X.

Procedure

The pitching machine should be preset to shoot fly balls in the direction of one of the cones. The speed control on the machine should be coordinated with the angle of the machine so that the balls consistently land within a 10-foot (3 m) radius of the cone.

   The game begins with an outfielder in ready position on the X in center field. As a coach or another player drops a ball into the pitching machine, the outfielder turns and sprints toward the cone to which the machine is aimed without looking back to the ball. When he nears the cone, he turns, finds the ball, and adjusts to make the catch. After the catch, another outfielder steps forward and assumes his ready position on the field, and the coach or player at the machine drops another ball into the machine. Play continues for as long as the coach desires.

Because pitching machines rarely throw the ball to the same spot in consecutive tosses, the outfielder will have to judge the speed and distance of the ball immediately as it leaves the machine. Outfielders can compete against each other, and points can be awarded for correctly judging the flight path of a ball and getting to the right location. After some practice with the cones in place, coaches can remove the cones and slightly adjust the speed of the pitching machine to create conditions that are more challenging and gamelike.

Coaching Points

- Make certain that outfielders execute good drop-step mechanics when they turn to go after a ball.
- Check that fielders catch the ball with their weight on the throwing-side foot with two hands above the throwing-side shoulder.

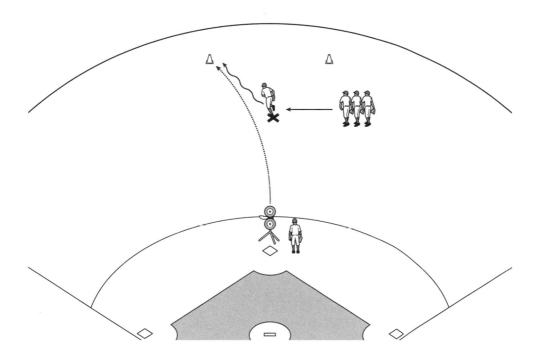

Tweeners

Age: *12 and older*   **Skill Level:** ◉◉◉◉

Introduction

This game is similar to Two-Line Communication (page 68) except that it employs the whole team. It gives outfielders work on coming in on popups and communicating with infielders and other outfielders. The game also helps validate the priority fielding system.

Equipment

Pitching machine or fungo hitter, baseballs

Setup

- ◉ Fielders assume their positions on the field.
- ◉ A fungo hitter or pitching machine is stationed at home plate.

Procedure

Players assume their ready positions. Play begins when the coach hits a popup or uses a machine to loft a popup between the outfield and the infield. Balls should be hit or lofted in a way that forces outfielders to charge hard and make decisions. If a machine is used, then at the same time a ball is placed in the machine, a batter standing nearby should take a swing to simulate a live event. When the ball is hit and an outfielder calls for it, the infielder should immediately move away from the area in a direction away from the flight of the ball. By varying the speed, direction, and angle of the pitching machine, coaches can give players practice in communicating about the many types of popups that occur in games. For example, aiming the machine to hit a high popup just fair or foul into the outfield behind first base engages three fielders—the first baseman, second baseman, and right fielder—who must try to get into position to make the catch. Runners can be placed on the bases to simulate game situations. Scoring for this game should be done on a team basis; points can be awarded for correct play or deducted for indecision.

Coaching Points

- Teach infielders simply to wave their hands above their heads to "call" for the ball.
- Teach shortstops and second basemen to be aggressive in going after popups near the foul lines behind third base and first base respectively.
- Make certain that catchers and pitchers move into appropriate backup positions on each play.

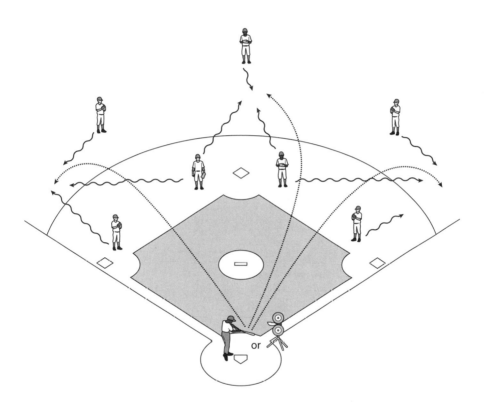

PITCHING GAMES

Diamond and One

Age: *12 and older*   **Skill Level:** ◉◉◉◉

Introduction

One of the greatest innovators in college basketball history was Marquette University coach Al McGuire. To contain high scorers from opposing teams, he devised the diamond-and-one defense—four players in a diamond playing zone defense and one chaser in the middle who hustled all over the floor following an opponent's ace. This game takes its name from that configuration but is adapted to a baseball field to give pitchers fielding practice. It resembles the basketball defense because the pitcher in the middle will be hustling all over fielding balls and throwing to all bases. The game prepares pitchers to approach balls properly, get their feet under their bodies quickly, and avoid rushing their throws. As an added benefit, the rapid pace of the game is an effective conditioner. I originally learned the basics of this game from Pat Daugherty, then the coach at Indian Hills (Iowa) Junior College and now special assistant to the general manager with the Colorado Rockies.

Equipment

Baseballs, throw-down bases or cones (if not using regular infield)

Setup

- The game requires five pitchers; if five are not available, fill in with position players.
- Use the infield, outfield grass, or other large open area. (The game can also be adapted to a gymnasium.)
- Use cones to represent bases or place throw-down bases in an infield configuration.

Procedure

If not using the regular infield, set up a diamond in a large open area with bases, if available, or cones. The game starts with pitchers at all four bases and one pitcher directly in the middle of the diamond. Assign one of the bases to be home plate. The pitcher in the middle, with a ball in hand, faces home, throws a pitch to the player there, and gets into fielding position. As soon as the player at home receives the ball, he immediately rolls it into the field and calls out a base at the same time. The pitcher in the middle fields the ball and throws to the base called.

Wherever the throw was made now becomes home. The pitcher sprints back to the original starting point, also possibly marked with a cone, and receives a return throw from the player with the ball. He throws another pitch to the base that is now home, and the player there rolls out the ball again and calls out another base. The game continues in this fashion for at least five throws, more if the coach desires. After the mandatory number of throws, another player goes to the middle and the game starts over.

Pitchers are scored on the number of accurate throws that they make. The receiving player should stand next to the cone and not move left or right to receive an errant throw. Points can be deducted for fielding errors or bad throws. Give incentives for winning.

The player receiving the pitch must call the base loudly and instantly so that the pitcher has time to align his body properly or circle the ball for the throw. Feeders should vary the speed of the balls that they throw, and they can throw line drives or popups as long as the throws are reasonably within the reach of the pitcher.

Coaching Points

- Make sure that pitchers step toward the base to which they are throwing, keeping their shoulders square and using good arm action.
- Players should barehand the ball only if it has stopped moving.
- On hard comebackers, teach pitchers to run the ball toward first base and underhand their throws.

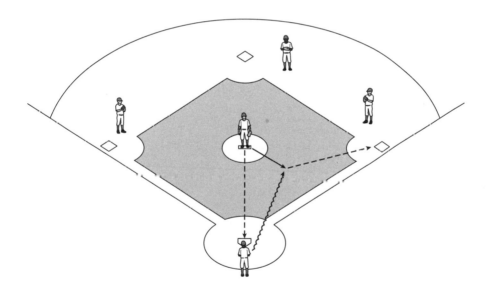

In the Box

Age: *12 and older*   **Skill Level:** 🟢🟢🟢🟢

Introduction

People often say that good pitchers need four things to be successful—velocity, movement, deception, and location. The following game concretely helps pitchers begin to understand the value of being able to place the ball in a desired location with each pitch. During preseason workouts, most coaches have pitchers chart pitches for each other—number of strikes, balls, fastballs, curves, and so forth. Pitchers should chart not only the number of strikes and types of pitches but also the location of pitches, from the first time that they throw to a catcher. Doing so helps them focus on the zones within the strike zone. The goal of this game is for pitchers to gain command of their pitches.

The pitching chart shown on the next page can be helpful in facilitating this understanding of location. It cuts the strike zone in half horizontally to differentiate pitches above the waist of the hitter from those below the waist. Pitchers need to keep most of their pitches down to be successful, and the chart helps them visualize this concept.

Equipment

Baseballs, clipboard, strike zone charts, pencils

Setup

- Use a bullpen or open area on the field.
- Catchers take positions behind home plates.
- Pitchers work in pairs. One pitcher sits in a chair charting pitches on a clipboard while the other throws.

Procedure

One pitcher throws his allotted pitches, and one pitcher sits behind him in a chair and marks the location of the pitches on the chart. A fresh chart should be used for each inning thrown (15 pitches). Catchers call balls and strikes, and the pitcher completing the chart makes a mark wherever the pitch was thrown. For simplicity, use a 1 for a fastball, 2 for a curve, 3 for a changeup, and so on (see figure). At the end of the bullpen session, the pitches should be totaled up and given a point value. For example, score one point for each pitch in zone 1 and two points for each pitch in zone 2. Any pitch outside the strike zone should be given three points. In this method of scoring, the lowest score is the best. Coaches should post results each day so that players can gauge their progress. Scoring adds an element of competition to an otherwise individual task.

Coaching Points

- Determine beforehand how many pitches the pitchers should throw from the windup or stretch.
- In addition, determine the types of pitches that they should throw.
- Be sure that pitchers focus on pitching mechanics at all times.

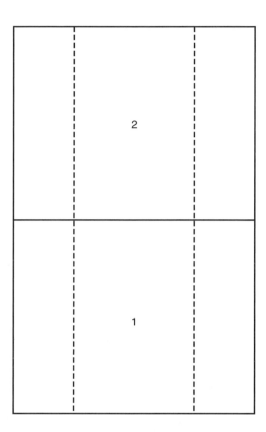

Location, Location, Location

Age: *12 and older*   **Skill Level:** 🔵🔵🔵🔵

Introduction

Just as in real estate, the key to good pitching has always been location. The history of baseball includes countless stories of pitchers who could not overwhelm hitters but were nonetheless extremely successful because they knew where to put the ball. Future Hall of Famer Gregg Maddux is an excellent example. Coaches are always searching for ways to keep their pitchers in the strike zone. This competitive game is a useful alternative to a bullpen session on an off day during the season. It allows pitchers to work on the location of their pitches while competing against a teammate in a gamelike setting.

Equipment

Baseballs, throw-down home plates

Setup

- Use an open area of the field near a fence (backstop).
- The game uses two catchers and two pitchers.

Procedure

This game should be played on flat ground to avoid straining the pitchers' arms. If only one catcher is available, pitchers should alternate throws.

Begin with the pitchers set up 40 feet (12 m) from their catchers. Each pitcher throws five pitches to his catcher from this distance and then moves back to 50 feet (15 m) away. After five throws at 50 feet, pitchers move back to 60 feet (18 m) and finally to 70 feet (20 m).

In the beginning of the season, or at the coach's discretion, pitchers may only throw fastballs. As the year progresses, various pitches should be included in the workout.

Catchers call each pitch a ball or a strike. Pitchers are scored by the number of strikes thrown. Records should be kept and scores posted. Coaches can decide the types of pitches thrown from each distance, but the last pitch of the five should always be a fastball because if pitchers can't throw fastballs for strikes, they'll never be successful.

Following is a sample progression: first five pitches—fastball, curveball, fastball, curveball, fastball; second five—fastball, curveball, fastball, curveball, fastball; and so on. Another variation might be to have pitchers throw fastball, curveball, changeup, curveball, fastball; fastball, etc.

This game motivates pitchers to do well because they are competing against their teammates and trying to prove that they can throw strikes with their whole repertoire. Because of the challenge involved, it also serves as a good alternative to a regular bullpen session.

Pitchers should work back to at least 70 feet (20 m) to stretch out their arm muscles, which leads to increased flexibility. Of course, with younger players, limit the distance to avoid straining their arms.

Another variation of this game would be to have pitchers start at 40 feet (12 m) and try to get 7 out of 10 pitches in the strike zone. Keep them throwing at this distance until they can do so. After they can, allow them to move back to 50 feet (15 m) and so on. This progression helps them focus on their delivery and release point.

Coaching Points

- Watch to be certain that mechanics stay the same from the varying distances, especially on the changeup and breaking balls.

- Some younger pitchers tend to push their changeups rather than throw them; from the longer distances they cannot do so.

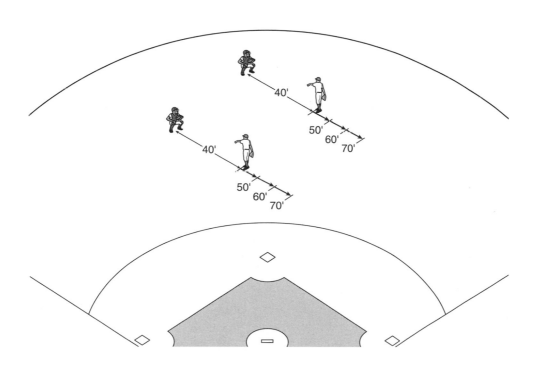

4.4 — **Pickoff Rotation**

Age: *12 and older*   **Skill Level:** 🔵🔵🔵🔵

Introduction

Most pitchers don't spend enough time working on holding runners on base, especially at the high school level. The following game takes only about 20 minutes to complete but allows an entire pitching staff to practice just about every pickoff situation in baseball as well as work on covering home plate after a wild pitch and throwing pitchouts.

Equipment

Bases, two baseballs per pitcher

Setup

- Use the dirt area around the pitcher's plate.
- Catcher is in position behind home plate.
- Fielders take all infield positions.
- Runners wearing helmets are at each base.

Procedure

Pitchers break into even groups surrounding the mound as shown in the figure. Pitchers on the first-base side of the mound throw to the first baseman, pitchers behind the mound work on pickoff plays with the shortstop and second baseman, pitchers on the third-base side of the mound throw to third base, and pitchers in front of the mound throw toward the catcher. After five or six throws each, pitchers rotate counterclockwise around the mound and the process begins again.

On the first-base side, pitchers work on a slow move and a quick move. Right-handed pitchers can work on throwing from different locations in their stretch motion and with varying rhythms according to what the coach believes is important. Left-handed pitchers can work on their deception and stepping on a 45-degree angle with the glove-side foot. On the second-base side, pitchers work with middle infielders on timing moves and on daylight plays. On the third-base side of the mound, pitchers work on stepping and throwing to third much as a left-hander does to first. They work on holding runners close and stepping on a 45-degree angle with the glove-side foot. On the home-plate side, pitchers can work on throwing pitchouts to the catcher and on covering the plate on wild pitches. The pitchout should be a good fastball thrown chest high to the catcher in the batter's box opposite the hitter. To facilitate the wild-pitch simulation, have the pitcher throw the ball over the head of the catcher and then sprint to home to cover the plate while the catcher retrieves the ball and throws it back to the pitcher.

Runners at each of the bases take leadoffs and serve as decoys for the pitchers. They should not dive back to the base but merely stand there to give the pitchers a more gamelike atmosphere. Pitchers can compete against each other by counting the number of accurate throws that they make. Four to eight pitchers works best for this game, but it can be played with only a few pitchers.

Coaching Points

◉ This game gives coaches an opportunity to teach a variety of moves that keep runners close to bases and put a damper on an opponent's aggressive running game. Many excellent sources discuss various moves to the bases and the way to teach them, including the book *Baseball Skills & Drills* by the American Baseball Coaches Association (Human Kinetics, 2001).

◉ Coaches should teach pitchers the proper technique for covering the plate on wild pitches or passed balls so that they can avoid injury.

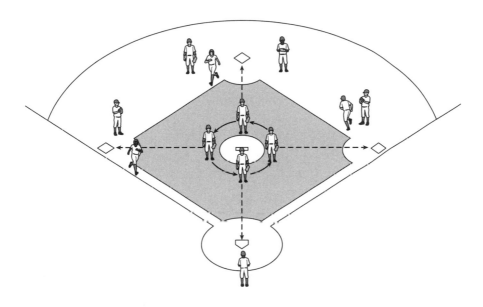

Pitcher's Duel

Age: *High school and older*   **Skill Level:** ●●●●

Introduction

Pitchers can play this game while working on their warm-up drills or during their practice sessions in the bullpen. The game helps pitchers focus on the strike zone and, more important, get the feel of moving the ball around the strike zone with all their pitches. Ideally, two pitchers should work together with one catcher, but if a catcher is not available, three pitchers can work together with one serving as the catcher. The game should take about 15 to 20 minutes per pitcher and should be played several times per week, especially early in the season. Keeping a tally of each pitcher's results in this game can be a good motivator that provides a needed early season challenge.

Equipment

Baseballs, gloves, clipboard, strike zone charts, pencils, chair, throw-down home plate (if game is played indoors or no bullpen is available)

Setup

◉ Two pitchers and one catcher are required (or three pitchers who alternate as the catcher).
◉ Pitchers should throw off flat ground when playing this game.
◉ The catcher and pitcher should be 45 feet (14 m) apart.
◉ The pitcher who isn't throwing sits off to the side and charts for his pitching teammate.

Procedure

Two pitchers should be paired together by ability level or age group. They should each throw two to three innings of 12 pitches each. The pitcher who isn't throwing charts the balls and strikes of the other pitcher. (Coaches should develop their own tracking method for this game, but a simple chart can be devised with rows for balls and strikes and columns for the different types of pitches.) Catchers determine whether a pitch is a strike or a ball. After each 12-pitch inning, players should rotate in order to game conditions.

Coaches should set up the throwing pattern based on what they think is important for the time of year and the players' stage of development. An example of a throwing pattern follows: first 12-pitch inning: 5 fastballs, 3 changeups, 2 breaking balls, 2 fastballs—all thrown from the windup position; second 12-pitch inning: 4 fastballs, 4 changeups, 4 breaking balls—all thrown from the stretch position.

Coaches might also have players switch from the windup to the stretch every two pitches, or they could choose to work one day on the windup only and then throw

98 | Pitching Games

from the stretch position the next day. Another option would be to work on only one pitch during a session and then work on a different pitch the next day.

Scoring: A basic tally of balls versus strikes could be used to determine the winner of the day's workout, or pitches could be weighted differently to reflect their degree of difficulty. For example, a curveball strike might count two points and a fastball as only one. Coaches can devise other scoring methods according to priorities. Charts should be posted to challenge pitchers to perform better.

Variation: Instead of just tracking balls and strikes, make the game more challenging by having pitchers throw to different locations within the strike zone. Players could be rated by the location of the ball in the strike zone using charts like those shown below. Mark the position of the pitch on the chart using a 1 for a fastball, 2 for a curve, 3 for a changeup, and so on.

Using the first chart, pitchers would be encouraged to throw only low strikes (zone 1) and receive credit only for balls thrown in that zone. With the second chart, they would have to move the ball from zone 1 to zone 2 to zone 3 in a pattern determined by the coach. Only balls thrown in those zones would receive credit.

Coaching Points

- Motivate players to improve each time by keeping records of past performance or by pitting pitchers against a performance goal.
- Coaches should be present when this game is played to watch mechanics closely.
- Always check balance, release points, follow-through, arm action, and so forth.

4.6 ── Smash Ball ─────

Age: *12 and older*   **Skill Level:** 🔵🔵🔵🔵

Introduction

A well-known pitching coach once said at a national clinic that pitchers should not be concerned about finishing their motion in good fielding position . . . because if they do, they had better be worried! His point was that pitchers should concentrate on throwing first because their job is to get the batter out. Fielding is secondary. But because pitchers are usually less than 55 feet (17 m) away from home when they finish their motion, they have to be able to shift from pitching mode to fielding mode quickly—sometimes in less than one-half second. This game gives pitchers practice in improving their reactions to hard-hit comebackers.

Equipment

Baseballs, rag balls, fungo bat

Setup

- Pitchers line up behind the mound.
- A catcher in full gear is behind home plate.
- A fielder is at first base.
- The coach stands with a fungo bat outside the batter's box with a bucket of soft-stitch baseballs. Many such balls are on the market.

Procedure

The first pitcher stands on the rubber with a ball in hand, goes through the pitching motion (windup or stretch), and throws a fastball to the catcher. When the ball is crossing the plate, the coach should hit a hard shot with a rag ball back at the pitcher. The pitcher should attempt to field the ball or knock it down, recover, and throw to first base.

After each throw, the pitcher returns to the end of the line and the next pitcher takes his position on the rubber.

Coaches should mix in bunts and high hoppers along with the hard smashes so that pitchers don't always expect hard-hit balls. Make the game into a competition among the pitchers to see who the best fielder is.

Coaching Points

○ Caution pitchers to get their bodies under control with their feet underneath their shoulders if possible before throwing.

○ Remind pitchers to use the crow hop when throwing so that they don't rush their throws. Many pitchers make errant throws when they hurry. They just field, stand up, and throw without moving their feet.

○ Make sure that pitchers use good throwing mechanics and don't shorten their pitching motion because they are concerned about fielding the smash coming their way.

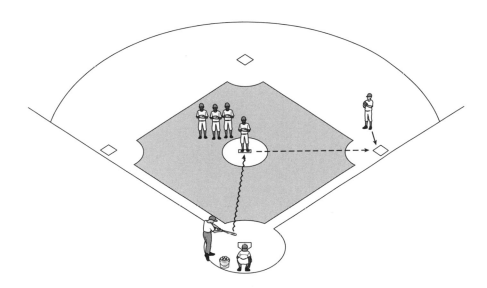

Dueling Pitchers (U-R-O-U-T)

Age: *12 and older*   **Skill Level:** 🔵🔵🔵🔵

Introduction

When pitchers work in the bullpen, they are rarely challenged to execute by situations when they must throw a strike. This game gives pitchers a chance to challenge each other one on one to see who has the best command of his pitches. Based on the playground basketball game H-O-R-S-E, this game should be the culmination of a pitcher's daily workout routine, especially in the preseason. When done regularly, it creates competitiveness among the pitching staff and a desire to succeed. It has the added benefit that it forces pitchers to throw pitches that they may not be comfortable throwing.

Equipment

Baseballs, clipboard, home plate

Setup

- Use a bullpen or an open area on the field.
- A catcher is in position behind the plate.

Procedure

Pitchers pair off and work together on their bullpen sessions. After completing their session, by prior agreement one pitcher throws the first ball in the game. Each pitcher in this two-person game calls his pitch, and his opponent must then duplicate it. For example, if the first pitcher calls a curveball, he must then throw that pitch. If the pitch is a strike, the second pitcher, his opponent, must throw the same pitch. If the second pitcher does not throw a strike with the curveball, he receives a letter. If the first pitcher does not throw a strike, the second pitcher may throw any pitch that he chooses but he must call it first. The game continues until one of the pitchers has accumulated all five letters: U-R-O-U-T. That pitcher is the loser.

With younger players, coaches may decide that throwing strikes with fastballs only is a sufficient challenge. The more accomplished the pitching staff is, the more sophisticated the game may become. For example, instead of just calling the pitch, players could also call the location—low, away, in, and so forth.

Pitchers could keep standings during the entire year and then present a suitable award at the end of the year to the pitcher with the most wins.

Coaching Points

- Coaches should make sure that players challenge each other enough by throwing all the pitches in their arsenals.
- This is a good time for pitchers to work on new pitches they have not yet mastered.

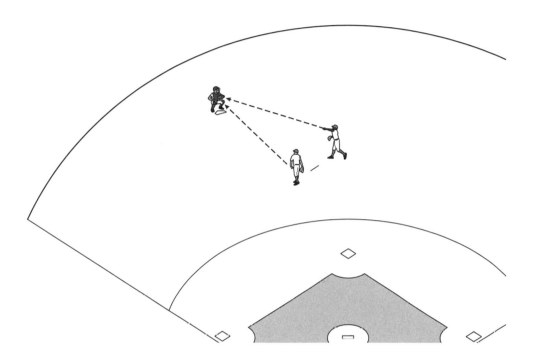

4.8 — **Pitching by Script**

Age: *12 and older* **Skill Level:** ⚾⚾⚾⚾⚾

Introduction

In the National Football League it has become fashionable for offensive coordinators to use a prescribed script at the beginning of games instead of calling plays one by one. They believe that a script enables a team to get all its options in motion early in a game. Furthermore, preparation is easy. Although the same approach may not be an option for a pitcher in the heat of a ballgame, scripting pitches at the end of a bullpen session allows pitchers to work on combinations that they may not think of in a game. The objective is to be able to command pitches, not necessarily throw strikes. The value of the game rests in its competitive atmosphere and the fact that it recreates game situations that may occur.

Equipment

Baseballs, clipboard, charts, throw-down home plates

Setup

- Use the bullpen or an open area of the field.
- Pitchers work in pairs.
- Two catchers are ready with their gear.

Procedure

If side-by-side bullpens are not available, use throw-down home plates and an area of the field with a backstop fence.

Pitchers work in pairs with one catcher. Two pitchers throw to one of the catchers; the other two pitchers throw to the other catcher. One pitcher keeps track of results, while the other throws. The game should be played at the end of a bullpen practice session and should follow any other work that pitchers may be doing. The routine should probably not involve throwing more than 10 or 12 pitches.

Pitchers are scored on the success of each pitch. An easy way to track pitches is to have a two-column form: One column lists the pitch thrown, and an adjacent column is used for the result. Use a plus sign (+) or a minus sign (–) for scoring. The chart on the next page provides an example. Again, posting results helps build staff awareness and challenges players to improve.

Coaches may set up any sequence that they wish and should vary the routine from session to session. Here is a sample sequence:

- Fastball inside to a right-handed batter (RH) for a strike
- Fastball low and away to a RH for a strike
- Fastball off the plate low and away to a RH

- Breaking pitch low and away to a RH for a strike
- Breaking pitch off the plate and away to a RH
- Fastball up and in to a RH; not necessarily a strike
- Changeup low and inside to RH for a strike
- Breaking pitch in the dirt and away to a RH
- 2-0 fastball (four seam) for a strike
- Breaking pitch for a strike

In this sequence, throwing a ball on pitch 1 and 2 would result in a negative point. Throwing a strike in pitch 3 would also be negative because the pitch called for is a setup pitch. In pitch 5, a breaking pitch anywhere but the prescribed location would be negative.

The possibilities with this game are endless. A pitcher's performance will be a good indicator of success in real games.

Coaching Points

- Watch to see that the pitcher's mechanics stay the same regardless of the pitch being thrown.
- Focus on the pitcher's linear alignment; the shoulder, head, hips, and glove should all be moving toward the target.

Script	Pitcher 1	Pitcher 2
Fastball, inside	+	−
Fastball, low and away	−	−
Fastball, off plate, low and away	+	−
Curveball, low and away, for strike	+	+
Curveball, off plate, low and away	−	−
Fastball, up and in	+	+
Changeup, low and in	−	−
Curveball, in dirt, away	+	−
Four-seam fastball, for strike	+	+
Curveball, for strike	+	−

Pick at Two

Age: *12 and older* **Skill Level:** ⚾⚾⚾⚾⚾

Introduction

Other than in drills, pitchers get little practice working on pickoffs to second base under gamelike conditions. As a result, they usually don't disguise their moves well or they telegraph them in some way. This game has multiple objectives. It allows pitchers opportunities to vary their moves, it gives middle infielders chances to work on their timing and bluffing when covering second, it gives runners opportunities to lengthen their leads in attempting to steal third, and it affords catchers the opportunity to work on their throws to third base.

Equipment

Baseballs

Setup

- Pitchers form a line on the right-field side of the mound.
- Fielders take positions at shortstop, second, and third.
- A batter is in the batter's box, switching from the left to the right side.
- A catcher in full gear is behind home plate.
- A line of runners is in short center field behind second base.
- A coach is in the third-base coaching box.

Procedure

Before starting, defensive and offensive players should devise signals for pickoffs and steals. They should not use normal team signs because then the runners will know what is happening. Play begins with one runner taking a primary lead at second base. The first pitcher in line assumes a position on the rubber, takes a sign, and comes set. Middle infielders work on their procedures for holding runners close. The pitcher has the option of throwing home or picking at second base. If the pitcher throws home, the runner must steal. Runners should be encouraged to increase their leads gradually to entice the pitcher to attempt pickoffs. Coaches should work on helping runners increase their leads.

Keep track of the number of pickoffs versus the number of steals. Give more points for a pickoff than for a steal to emphasize the defense.

Coaching Points

○ Make certain that pitchers vary their looks to second base. They can look home and throw to second, look to second and throw home, look to second and throw to second, and so on.

○ Teach pitchers to use different rhythms. They can pause for long periods at times, step off at other times, and sometimes throw home quickly.

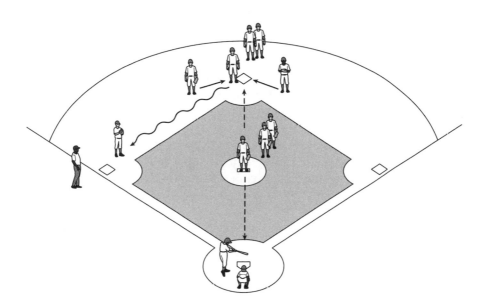

4.10

In and Out, Up and Down

Age: *High school and older*   **Skill Level:** 🟤🟤🟤🟤🟤

Introduction

This game is an advanced version of In the Box (page 92) that should be used only with older pitchers. The first chart shown on the next page, drawn for a pitcher facing a right-handed batter, divides the strike zone into four parts, each numbered according to its relative significance in the scheme of pitching. For left-handed batters the numbers would be reversed. Zones 1 and 2 are the zones that coaches want pitchers to throw into most often. Zone 3 signifies a high and tight pitch that all good pitchers need to learn to throw. Zone 4 is no man's land, the place where pitchers never want to throw the ball! Pitchers who put a ball in that zone should say, "Sayonara."

The second chart shown raises the difficulty by increasing the number of zones to nine. This version of the game demands far more subtlety and finer degree of control from the pitcher. Because of the high level of skill required to have success with this chart, it should only be used by the most experienced pitchers.

Equipment

Baseballs, clipboard, strike zone charts, pencils

Setup

- Use a bullpen or an open area on the field.
- Catchers are in position behind home plates.
- Pitchers pair up. One pitcher sits in a chair charting pitches on a clipboard while the other throws.

Procedure

One pitcher throws his allotted pitches, and the other pitcher sits behind him in a chair and marks the location of the pitches on the chart. A fresh chart should be used for each inning thrown (15 pitches). Catchers call each pitch a ball or a strike, and the pitcher completing the chart makes a mark where the pitch was thrown. For simplicity, use a 1 for a fastball, 2 for a curve, 3 for a changeup, and so on. At the end of the bullpen session, the pitches should be totaled up and given a point value. For example, pitches in zone 1 are worth one point, pitches in zone 2 are worth two points, and so on. Any pitch outside the strike zone should be given five points. As with In the Box, the lowest score is the best. Coaches should post results each day so that players can gauge their progress. Coaches can devise their own scoring method, but any pitch in zone 4 should be given a greater penalty because those are the mistake pitches that good hitters clobber. Perhaps those pitches could be given six points because in some ways they can be worse than throwing a ball. Employ a similar scoring method if using the second chart.

Coaching Points

○ Determine beforehand how many pitches should be thrown from the windup or stretch; determine as well how many fastballs, curves, and so on should be thrown.

○ With the four-zone chart, coaches can also devise patterns for pitchers. For example, pitchers could throw one pitch to zone 3, the next to zone 1, and then another to zone 3. Scoring could be changed to reward pitchers who are able to work successfully within the pattern.

9	8	5
7	6	4
3	2	1

4	3
2	1

CATCHING GAMES

Catcher Challenge

Age: *12 and older*   **Skill Level:**

Introduction

In old-school baseball, the biggest and slowest players on the team were turned into catchers. Not anymore. The catcher may be the most important player on the team. He must be agile and quick, as well as intelligent. This game helps catchers develop the quick reactions they need to receive or block pitches and react to game situations.

Equipment

Bucket of baseballs, catcher's gear, home plate, cones

Setup

- Catchers in full gear work in pairs.
- One catcher in full gear is behind home plate.
- Cones mark the game area.

Procedure

Players in full catcher's gear partner up. They both assume receiving position 6 feet (1.8 m) apart. Place four markers around each catcher, creating a 4-foot-by-4-foot (1.2 by 1.2 m) square. One catcher is the feeder and tries to get the ball past the other catcher using underhand throws. He must throw the ball below head level. The receiving catcher uses good blocking or receiving technique to block or catch balls and keep them within the marked area. After the receiver has 10 chances, the players switch roles. If equipment is not available for both catchers to be in full gear, one can be a regular feeder and the other the catcher. Softie balls or Wiffle balls may be substituted for baseballs.

The feeder receives two points for a successfully passed ball and one point for a blocked ball that travels outside the zone (4-foot-by-4-foot square). The receiving catcher earns one point for each caught ball or blocked ball that stays in the zone.

Coaches can add an additional challenge to the game by placing another fielder 75 feet (23 m) from home plate. On each ball fed, the receiving catcher has to get into throwing position and throw to the fielder. Points can be added for accurate throws.

Coaching Points

- Catchers must be in the ready-to-throw position when receiving. Don't let them become lazy and sit on their haunches.
- Watch to make certain that they soften their upper bodies when blocking balls.

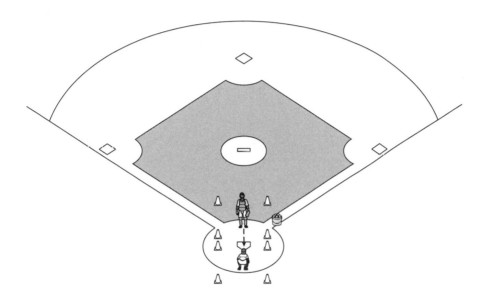

5.2 —— **Fielding Bunts** ——

Age: _10 and older_   Skill Level: 🏐🏐

Introduction

Besides calling pitches and controlling the flow of a game, a catcher must be able to field his position. Catchers have to be ready to pounce on bunted balls and make plays at the bases with strong, accurate throws. The following game provides practice on correct fielding of bunts to all locations. When played daily, it gives catchers work on their throwing footwork, scooping the ball, and getting the ball in proper throwing position.

Equipment

Bucket of baseballs, catcher's gear, home plate

Setup

- A catcher in gear is behind home plate.
- A coach stands directly behind the catcher.
- A fielder is at first base, second base, and third base.
- The bucket of baseballs should be within easy reach of the coach.

Procedure

The catcher, in full gear, assumes an upright receiving position behind home plate as if he were about to receive a pitch with a runner on base. The coach standing behind the catcher rolls a ball between the catcher's legs to simulate a bunted ball. With each rolled ball, the coach should call out the base to which the ball should be thrown. The catcher should move quickly to the ball, scoop it with both hands, get his feet underneath him, transfer his body into throwing position, and throw to the base. After each ball is rolled, the catcher returns to receiving position behind home plate and another ball is rolled in the same fashion. Balls should be rolled left, right, and straight ahead of the catcher with varying speeds to simulate all types of bunts. Coaches can alternate to which base the catcher throws, but with less experienced players, most throws should be directed to first base. As catchers become more accomplished, they can make throws to other bases. To challenge the catcher, the coach could call out the situation before rolling the ball. For example, he might say, "Runner on second base, no outs." Then the catcher can be scored on his judgment as well as his fielding and throwing ability. Points can be awarded for fielding the ball cleanly and making good throws. When other bases become part of the scenario, the coach can award or deduct points for making sound decisions after fielding the ball. For example, with a runner on second the catcher may field a bunt and throw to third base. But if the coach deems that the catcher, based on the speed of the ball and how far he had to go to field it, should have made the throw to first instead, points can be deducted from his daily total.

The catcher should field at least five bunts during the game. As with other contests, a daily record gives the game more validity and keeps catchers competitive.

Coaching Points

- Check that catchers are using a scooping technique—fielding the ball with both hands.
- Watch closely to see that the transfer from fielding to throwing position is quick and smooth.
- Make certain that catchers maintain their balance and throw overhand.

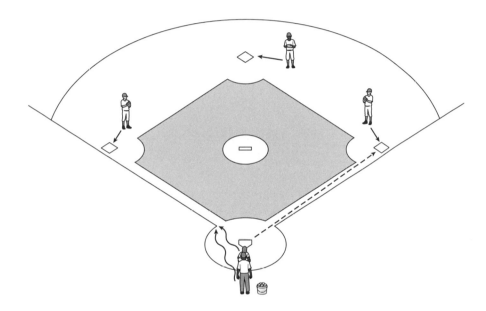

5.3 — **Guard the Castle**

Age: *10 and older*   **Skill Level:** 🥎🥎

Introduction

Although wild pitches are credited to pitchers, catchers should have the frame of mind that they should prevent any ball from going past them. One way to get catchers into this mind-set is to convince them that they are guardians of the area around home plate, that this area is their castle. In medieval times, knights had the responsibility of keeping threats out of the castle; in baseball, the catcher's task is to keep things in! The following game should be practiced each day to some extent. It gives catchers daily work in the fundamentals of blocking balls in the dirt and provides an element of competition at the same time. When worked into a catcher's daily routine, it should take only five minutes. This game is similar to the infielder game of Goalie (page 48) but uses a more confined area.

Equipment

10 baseballs, 10 Wiffle balls, ball bucket, catcher's gear, home plate

Setup

- Catchers pair off 25 feet (8 m) apart.
- Cones mark the game area.
- One catcher in full gear is behind home plate.
- The other catcher serves as the feeder facing the first catcher.
- A bucket of balls should be within easy reach of the feeder.

Procedure

One catcher, in full gear, assumes a receiving position behind home plate; the other catcher is the feeder and stands facing the receiving catcher from about 25 feet (8 m) away. The feeder throws balls into the dirt to the left and right of home plate. (Feeders should practice randomly throwing balls to the left and right of home plate to learn the proper spin necessary for imitating curveballs in the dirt.) Cones should be used to mark the area within which the balls should be thrown—to begin with, 4 feet (1.2 m) on either side of home plate. After blocking the ball, the receiving catcher returns to position and awaits the next ball. As soon as he is back in balanced receiving position, the feeder throws another ball. After 10 repetitions, catchers should switch positions.

Each ball thrown within the area delineated by the cone that gets through or past the receiving catcher counts as a point scored for the feeder. Balls that the catcher blocks but that bounce outside the cone area also count as a point for the feeder. Each catcher should perform the drill twice. Daily scores could be posted or kept on a clipboard in the dugout.

Coaching Points

- Coaches should make certain that catchers use good blocking technique and do not simply reach for the ball with their gloves.
- Because catchers often do not correctly angle their bodies toward home plate when blocking, emphasis should be placed on keeping the ball in front of the plate after blocking it.

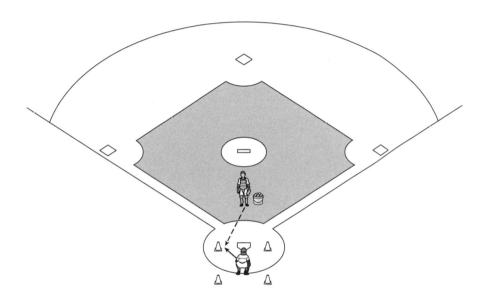

5.4 — Sway and Frame

Age: *10 and older*   Skill Level: ●●

Introduction

Catchers need to be schooled in correct receiving mechanics so that they can frame pitches and help pitchers get more called strikes. This game helps catchers develop good hand reactions and the ability to sway the body rather than jerk it, which helps an umpire see a pitch as a strike. The game can be played in 10 minutes. The game requires two players or two players and a coach.

Equipment

10 baseballs, 10 Wiffle balls, empty ball bucket, catcher's gear, home plate

Setup

- ◉ Catchers pair off.
- ◉ The receiving catcher is in full gear is behind home plate.
- ◉ Place an empty bucket to the glove side of the receiving catcher.
- ◉ The other catcher faces the receiving catcher at a distance of 15 feet (5 m) and serves as the feeder.

Procedure

One catcher assumes a receiving position behind home plate wearing no glove and holding his throwing hand behind his back. The other catcher tosses Wiffle balls underhand from 15 feet (5 m) away to various locations in and out of the strike zone—in, out, up, and down. After the catcher receives the ball, he quickly puts it in the empty bucket to his left and then reassumes the receiving position. As soon as the catcher is back in balanced receiving position, the feeder tosses another ball to him. After 10 tosses the players switch positions. After 10 or 20 catches with the Wiffle balls, the catcher puts his glove on his receiving hand and repeats the drill—this time using real baseballs (see figure). Tosses should be done rapid fire so that catchers only have time to react. In addition, locations should be opposites for optimum effect, that is, the first ball should be up and in, the second ball should be down and away, the third ball should be up and away, and so on.

Catchers are scored on their ability to react and get the receiving hand into proper position on each throw—thumb down for balls to the right of the plate, thumb up for balls to the left, and so forth. Catchers are also scored on whether they keep their noses above the ball and how well they sway their bodies in reaction to the throws. One point given for each correctly framed ball. This game should be a daily competition for catchers. If a team has only one catcher, the coach or a designated player should assist daily.

Coaching Point

● Coaches should check to make sure catchers are swaying using their ankles and not just lunging and grabbing with their arms.

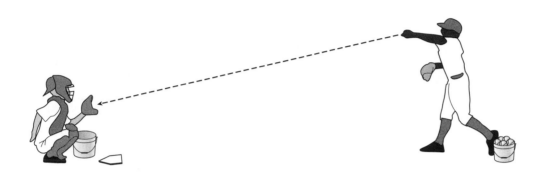

5.5 — Egg Drop

Age: *12 and older*   **Skill Level:** 🥎🥎🥎🥎

Introduction

Blocking a ball is only part of what catchers need to do with balls in the dirt. They also need to block the ball softly so that they can pounce on it and be ready to throw if a base runner tries to advance. The objective of this game is to teach catchers to soften up their bodies while blocking, quickly scoop up the loose ball, and get into throwing position. I am grateful to my coaching friend Ron Davini of Arizona, former baseball coach at Corona del Sol High School and now the executive director of the National High School Baseball Coaches Association, for the progression of blocking skills detailed here. When worked into a catcher's daily skill set, this game provides effective practice in keeping balls within the catcher's castle.

Equipment

Bucket of baseballs, catcher's gear

Setup

- A catcher in full gear is behind home plate.
- Other catchers are stationed off to the side of the plate awaiting their turns.
- A coach is stationed 25 feet (8 m) in front of home plate between the pitcher's mound and home.
- A bucket of balls is next to the coach.
- Optional: An infielder is covering second base.

Procedure

Before playing the game, coaches should instruct their catchers in basic softening technique. Coaches can do this by having their catchers line up in receiving stance along the third- or first-base line. The coach gives them a series of five commands, and they perform the skills together. Following is the progression of commands and the technique to be practiced for each command. (1) *Drop*: The catcher's shinguards must drop flat on the ground. The weight must be back, not on the knees. The shoulders must be square to the ball, and the eyes must be tracking the ball. Both hands drop to the ground, and the fingers are pointing toward the dirt. Catchers should try to plant their fingers into the ground. (2) *Blow*: When the knees and hands drop, the catchers must blow out all the air in their lungs. Convince them that they are making themselves into a big soft pillow. (3) *Curl*: This action occurs naturally when catchers blow out the air. Their shoulders curl forward, helping to form the body into a reverse C shape. (4) *Pop*: After they have dropped and released the air, they should pop back up onto their feet by pushing up with their knees and hands. (5) *Fetch*: As quickly as they can, they need to field the ball.

The game begins with one catcher behind home plate in full gear. The coach throws a ball into the dirt at the catcher. The catcher drops, blows, curls, pops, and fetches the ball, bringing the ball and his body into throwing position. After doing this, he drops the ball to the ground next to him and resumes his catching stance. The coach then fires another ball into the dirt, and the two of them repeat the process at least four more times. When the coach has finished with the catcher, depending on the location and direction of the blocked balls, the catcher may be quite a distance from home plate and the balls left behind may look like something out of an Easter egg hunt. Repeat the drill with the second catcher.

Because the game is demanding, coaches should give catchers a rest after five balls in the dirt. Coaches can devise their own scoring system to rate catchers against one another. For example, players can be timed with a stopwatch to see how fast they can accomplish the blocking of the five balls.

After players become proficient, coaches could add a new wrinkle and let the catchers throw to second base after they have fetched the ball.

Working daily with this game teaches catchers that even if they fail to catch a pitch, they can throw runners out if they are soft in their blocking technique. In high school, runners, even when they are trying to advance, tend to relax somewhat on balls in the dirt. Catchers who are quick to pounce and throw can cut down runners and discourage even the most aggressive teams.

During the season, a coach can even keep track of a new stat—bases saved—by tallying the number of times that a catcher blocks a ball in the dirt and keeps a runner from advancing. This stat would give catchers more incentive to become good blockers.

Coaching Points

- When they are in the drop mode, make sure that catchers plant the fingers of both hands straight into the ground.
- Watch to see that catchers do not try to catch the ball in the dirt.
- Caution catchers to use the scoop technique when fetching the ball in the dirt.

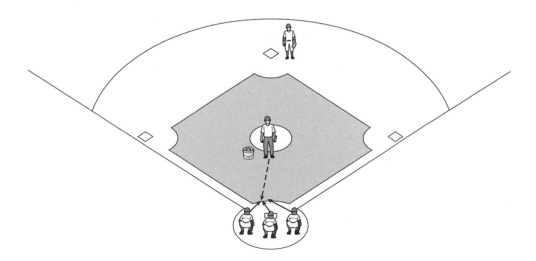

Tag and Score

Age: *12 and older*   **Skill Level:** ⚾⚾⚾⚾

Introduction

Coaches often pay little attention to the ability of catchers to make tags on runners on throws from the outfield. Often, the skill is practiced only during pregame infield practice when infielders throw to the plate and catchers practice tagging phantom runners. This game gives catchers real-time practice in getting ready to receive a throw, blocking the plate, and making tags. In addition, it provides opportunities for players to make decisions about whether to slide or to stand up.

Equipment

Bucket of baseballs, catcher's gear, pitching machine, blanket (for indoor use)

Setup

- A line of runners stands at third base.
- A catcher in full gear, minus mask, stands in front of the plate.
- A first baseman is stationed in cut position near the pitcher's mound.
- Other catchers are stationed off to the side of the plate awaiting their turns.
- A coach and pitching machine are located in the shallow outfield.
- A bucket of balls is near the coach.
- A player acting as the on-deck hitter is 15 feet (5 m) behind home plate in line with the foul line.

Procedure

The catcher assumes a position in front of the plate facing the direction from which the ball will come. The pitching machine should be set in center or right field and aimed so that it throws a one- or two-hop throw to the plate. The speed of the machine should be adjusted so that it approximates the average outfielder's throwing speed. The first runner in line assumes a tag-up position at third base.

The game begins when the runner at third tags and sprints toward home plate. As soon as the runner leaves the base, the coach drops a ball into the machine. The catcher watches the ball into his glove. If the throw arrives before the runner does, the catcher blocks the plate and uses good tag mechanics to tag the runner. If the throw is off line or late, the catcher may have to use a sweep tag to make the play. The on-deck hitter standing behind the plate in line with the play must use oral and visual signals to the runner coming down the line to indicate whether he should slide or stand up. After the runner scores or is out, he trades places with the on-deck hitter, who goes to the end of the line at third base. The next runner in the line assumes a tag position, and play begins again.

Coaches can adjust the speed of the machine with each throw or slightly alter the aim to reflect gamelike conditions more closely. A first baseman can cut off-line throws and make relays to the catcher. Catchers will get practice in making the decision to have the first baseman cut the ball or let it go through. They also learn how to block and hold on to the ball when applying tags. Players acting as on-deck hitters get experience in reading when to tell a player to slide or not.

The game could pit the offense versus the defense. Points can be awarded for each correct performance or decision—using proper sliding technique, holding on to the ball, deciding whether to cut the ball or let it go through, making the right decision as the on-deck hitter, and so forth.

This game works well in a gymnasium in inclement weather. When done indoors, a small blanket should be laid on the floor about 10 feet (3 m) up the line from home plate. Runners from third start their slides on the blanket, and the blanket itself will slide along the floor, preventing runners from getting sliding burns. Instead of using a pitching machine, coaches could throw the balls home from various angles on the floor, reproducing all the variations that might occur in a ball game—low throws, high throws, one-bounce throws, throws on the fly, and so on. A cutoff would not be necessary in a gym.

Coaching Points

- Remind players to assume an athletic position with the knees bent while awaiting the ball.
- Make certain that when catchers are blocking the plate, they have the left foot on the left-field foul line and point the toes directly toward third base. Injuries can occur if the foot is opened or closed along that line.
- Remind catchers to grab the ball firmly with the throwing hand and use both hands to make tags. Holding the ball this way keeps it more secure and helps prevent sliding runners from dislodging it.
- Caution runners to slide into home plate feet first. Do not allow headfirst slides when the catcher is blocking the plate.

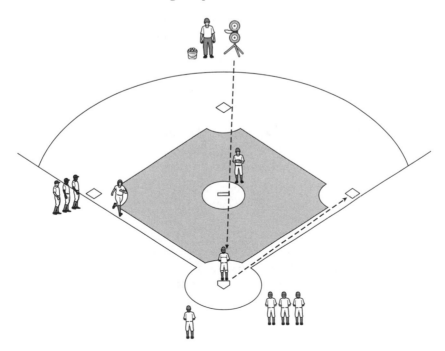

Transfer and Let It Fly

Age: *12 and older*   **Skill Level:** 🏐🏐🏐🏐

Introduction

When runners reach base, catchers have to be ready to throw after receiving every pitch. And although throwing technique is important, even more important is being able to transfer the ball quickly from the catcher's mitt to the throwing hand and make the throw. Some say that the catcher's throw is the most violent in baseball because the throw of more than 127 feet (38 m) must be made almost from a dead stop with little time to think about mechanics. This game helps catchers become more adept at what might be the most important aspect of the throw—transferring the ball from the glove to the throwing hand. The objective of this game is to get catchers to quicken their release time while maintaining their throwing accuracy.

Equipment

Bucket of baseballs, catcher's gear, Softhands training glove (or similar device), small mat, catcher's mitt

Setup

- A catcher in full gear takes a position on the first-base line about halfway between home and first.
- A coach stands parallel to the first catcher in foul territory.
- A bucket of balls is within easy reach of the coach.
- A fielder takes a position along the first-base line near first base.
- Have a stopwatch available to time the catcher's throws.

Procedure

A catcher in full gear kneels on one knee about 45 feet (15 m) from home plate. His right knee should be on the ground along the foul line, and his left foot should be on the foul line pointed toward first base. The catcher should have a Softhands glove on his catching hand. His throwing hand should be next to the Softhands glove in good receiving position, and his shoulders should be parallel to the foul line for the start of the game. His hands should be situated near the center of his chest. He should be kneeling upright, not on his haunches.

A coach should be in foul territory about 15 feet (5 m) from the catcher and the same distance from home plate. The game begins when the coach takes a ball from the bucket and tosses it hard underhand toward the catcher's midsection. Without getting up, the catcher catches the ball in the Softhands glove, immediately transfers it to the throwing hand, brings the hand up into throwing position, and fires to the fielder standing near first base.

Repeat this routine five times and then switch catchers.

Catchers can be scored on how smoothly and quickly they transfer the ball and make the throw. A stopwatch could be used to add a challenge to the game and give catchers a measure by which they can rate their development. Post times often.

As players become accustomed to the game, coaches can gradually lengthen the distance. Progressing in 10-foot (3 m) increments allows players to maintain their skill level while increasing the degree of difficulty.

After a few rounds with the Softhands glove, catchers should switch to a real catcher's mitt and repeat the process. When working on this game with younger players, shorten the distance at first to make it more compatible with the distance between bases in youth leagues. Players can kneel on a small gym mat to help save their knees from fatigue.

Coaching Points

- ● Make sure that the catchers turn the wrist of the glove hand after receiving the ball to ease the transfer to the throwing hand.
- ● Make sure that they rotate their shoulders and follow through on each throw.
- ● Watch that the throwing-arm elbow is above the throwing-arm shoulder. As the game distance becomes longer, place more emphasis on proper throwing mechanics.

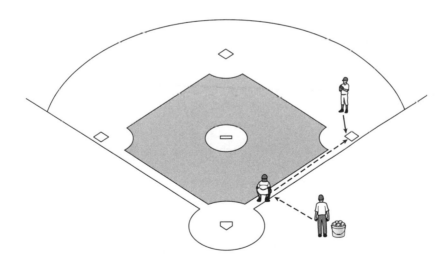

5.8 — Wild Pitch

Age: *12 and older*   **Skill Level:** ●●●●

Introduction

Pitchers should always be more focused and careful when a runner is on third base. A mistake pitch in this situation can result in an easy run for the opposition. Catchers also have to be more intent on guarding their castle when a runner is only one base away. Mistakes do occur, however, leading to scrambling situations and plays at the plate. This game serves many purposes. It gives catchers practice in retrieving wild pitches or passed balls, it provides pitchers with chances to cover home plate, and it presents base runners with opportunities to be aggressive and try to score. It also creates a challenging atmosphere between the base runners and the defense.

Equipment

Baseballs, catcher's gear

Setup

- Put a line of runners at third base.
- A batter is in the batter's box and occasionally switches from hitting right-handed to hitting left-handed.
- A coach stands 15 feet (5 m) behind the catcher with several balls in hand.
- A pitcher is on the mound and a catcher in full gear takes a position behind the plate.
- Optional: Place a runner at first base, a shortstop in normal position, and a third baseman in normal position.

Procedure

Start by having the pitcher simulate a pitch and have the catcher drop to his blocking position. When the catcher drops to block, the coach, who is standing in the area behind home plate, tosses a ball somewhere behind the plate to the left or right. The catcher must quickly pop up, turn, retrieve the ball, and throw to the pitcher who covers the plate.

The runner at third base should have a three-step lead. When the coach tosses the ball, the runner breaks for home plate to try to score. After each out or run scored, the runner takes the place of the batter. The batter goes to the end of the line of runners at third, and play continues.

Award the defense 2 points for every out offense 1 point for each score. The first group to score 10 points wins. The coach can make the game more or less difficult depending on where and how hard he tosses the ball.

Catchers, pitchers, runners, and batters should be rotated often to give everyone work. If necessary, coaches could prohibit sliding to lessen the chance for injury.

Variation: Place a runner at first base and fielders at third and short. On each simulated wild pitch, the shortstop breaks quickly for the mound area to back up the pitcher and the runner at first tries to get to third base. Catchers have the option of throwing to third if they have no play on the runner coming home, or in the event of a wild throw by the catcher, the shortstop retrieves the ball and tries to stop the runner from reaching third base.

Coaching Points

- Teach catchers the proper way to retrieve balls, including having them slide while fielding the ball.
- Teach pitchers the proper way to cover the plate. They must break hard to the plate and slow down before they get there to avoid crossing the plate or being in line with the runner.
- Instruct pitchers to yell while running and point in the direction of the ball to help the catcher.

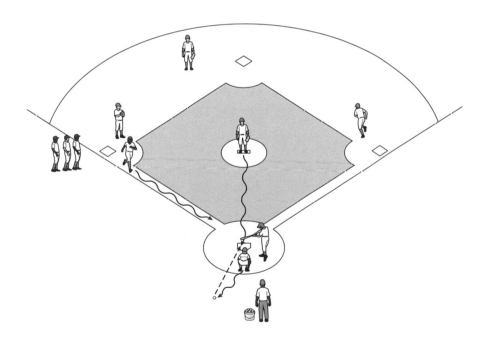

Pick 'Em

Age: *12 and older* **Skill Level:** ◉◉◉◉◉

Introduction

Many coaches are reluctant to have their catchers throw to the bases because of the possibility of throwing errors, especially when a runner is on third base because a mistake in that situation leads to a run. The demands of practice normally leave little time for catchers to work on their pickoff skills. This game, which can easily be played in five minutes each day, gives catchers opportunities to sharpen their throwing skills to first base and third base. It enables them to work on quickening their feet and rapidly transferring the ball from mitt to hand. The key objective is for catchers to make accurate throws to the bases.

Equipment

Cones (tall, if available), baseballs, stopwatch

Setup

- Cones are targets in this game, so use tall ones if available.
- Catchers form a line behind home plate.
- A first baseman and third baseman are at their positions.
- A batter is in the batter's box.
- A feeder or coach stands 20 feet (6 m) in front of home plate.

Procedure

Place cones on both sides of both first base and third base. One cone should be touching the base in foul territory; the other should be no more than 1 foot (30 cm) inside the base parallel to the first cone. These become targets or goals for the catchers. The first and third basemen should be in ready position on the infield grass a few feet (a meter or so) from the foul line. The batter in the box (who does not swing) switches sides after each throw. The catcher is in receiving position behind the plate.

Play begins when the coach or feeder throws a fastball at moderate speed to the catcher. As the ball is thrown, the coach should clearly call the base to which the catcher should throw by saying, for example, "First, first, first." The catcher should execute the throwing techniques taught by the coach and throw to the base called. Catchers should aim the ball at the goal formed by the two cones at the base. Fielders catch the throws and return the ball to the coach or feeder. Using the cones reminds catchers that their throws will be more effective when kept lower. Give each catcher three throws before switching catchers.

Coaches can devise their own scoring method but should generally follow this format: Balls thrown within the area bounded by, and no higher than, the cones receive five points; balls in the general vicinity but too high or outside the goal earn three points; and any ball that a fielder has to reach for receives one point. Deduct points for wild throws.

Each throw should also be timed with a stopwatch. Keep records and post them to add an element of competition.

Coaching Points

- Remind catchers not to sit on their haunches and to be in the up position when receiving with runners on base.
- Introduce the knee-drop pickoff throw to first for catchers with strong arms. Because many catchers drop to their knees when returning the ball to the pitcher, runners can be lulled into thinking that the catcher won't pick when doing this.
- Teach catchers to swing the left knee in the direction of first base just before it hits the ground and to rifle the ball to first. A good throw can catch runners napping.
- Frequently review the catcher's footwork, transference of the ball, and arm action.

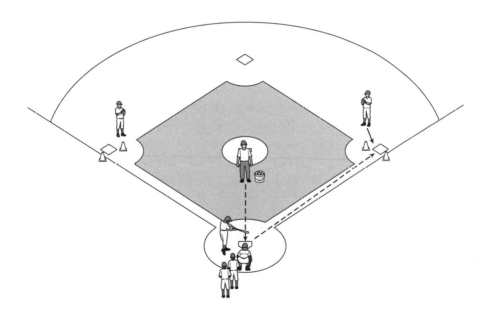

Rapid Fire

Age: *12 and older*   **Skill Level:** 🌑🌑🌑🌑

Introduction

Although the strike zone is clearly defined in the rule book, no coach—or umpire, for that matter—would deny the fact that the way a catcher frames a ball has an effect on whether a pitch is called a ball or a strike. Catchers need to be able to move their mitts smoothly and quickly to a position that helps influence the pitch call so that it favors the pitcher. The objective of this game is to give catchers practice in changing their hand position rapidly and catching balls moving from one side of the plate to the other. It helps catchers speed up their reaction time and serves as a good conditioner.

Equipment

Two buckets of baseballs, catching gear, pitching machine (optional)

Setup

- Catchers in full gear are behind home plate.
- Two pitchers are 45 feet (15 m) from the plate.
- Optional: Set up a pitching machine in front of the mound.

Procedure

Two pitchers, or coaches, stand about 45 feet (15 m) from home plate and about 5 feet (1.5 m) apart. Place a bucket of balls next to each pitcher. A catcher, in full gear, sits in receiving position behind the plate. One pitcher goes through the pitching motion and delivers a pitch to the catcher. After he receives the ball, the catcher tosses it to the side and gets ready to receive again. When the catcher receives the ball from the first pitcher, the second pitcher starts his pitching motion and throws another pitch. The catcher catches it, tosses it aside, and gets ready for another pitch. The game continues in this fashion, with pitchers alternating throws, for 10 pitches. After 10 pitches, switch catchers and continue.

Catchers can be graded on how quickly they rotate the mitt to react to a pitch's location and how well they frame the ball. Pitchers can throw any pitch—fastball, curve, or changeup—to a variety of locations in the zone, although starting with strictly fastballs is best until catchers have gained some proficiency with their gloves. This game can become a good ball-in-the-dirt reaction drill as well, but caution pitchers not to throw until the catcher is ready to receive.

If coaches have access to a pitching machine that is easily adjustable, such as the ATEC Rookie or similar devices, it can be used in place of two pitchers. But using pitchers gives them practice in consistently hitting the strike zone.

Coaching Points

- Make certain that the catcher doesn't reach for the pitch. He should sway to keep his nose over the ball.
- Remind catchers to catch the outside part of the ball or the top of the ball, depending on pitch location.
- Grade catchers on how quickly they rotate their mitts to react to the location of the pitch and how well they frame the ball.

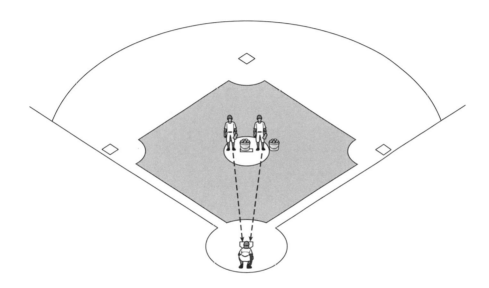

HITTING GAMES

Target Hitting

Age: *10 and older*   **Skill Level:** *All*

Introduction

A staple of every coach's daily plan is batting practice. Although using tees to teach and hone hitting skills has become almost ritualistic, many players just don't take hitting drills off tees seriously. Young players hitting off a batting tee don't really pay attention to where the ball is going or even what part of the bat hits the ball—they just try to hit it! This game, when played every day at practice, forces players to concentrate on hitting the ball on the sweet spot and creates a lively, competitive atmosphere out of what has become routine for many. Other games in this book recommend using daily measurements; with this game measuring and accounting are required!

Equipment

Baseballs, batting tee, target net, clipboard, charts

Setup

- ◉ Have players pair up.
- ◉ Set up batting tees along the batting cage or portable sock hitting nets.
- ◉ A dozen baseballs should be placed at each station.
- ◉ Have a clipboard and pencils available near the tee.

Procedure

Coaches can set up tee stations anyway they prefer—along fencing, with sock nets, outside a batting-tunnel net, and so on. At each station, coaches should either make targets that hang on the netting or use paint or tape to mark areas of the netting as target areas. Targets can be any dimension a coach deems suitable for a particular age group or skill level. The targets can be circular, rectangular, or square. The key is that they should not be too big and should provide an area within which players are trying to hit the ball off the tee. An area 2 1/2 feet by 3 feet (75 by 90 cm) would be large enough. In addition, tees should not be too close to the target area. Players should carry with them a daily hitting chart on which they mark their scores on each hitting station. If players work in pairs, partners can mark the score for each other. A simple chart with boxes for each day of the week and each hitting station—soft toss, tees, live, top-hand tee swings, and so on—would be sufficient.

Play begins when the feeder places a ball on the tee and the batter swings. After each swing, the feeder places another ball on the tee, and the batter swings again. After five swings, the feeder marks on the batter's chart the number of times that player A hit the ball into the target area. Points can be given for balls hit into the target area—one ball, one point. Then the players reverse roles and begin again. After each round of five swings, the tee should be moved in relation to the target to simulate inside pitches, pitches over the middle, and outside pitches.

Players charts should be collected periodically, and their aggregate scores should be posted in a prominent place to provide incentive for improvement. As players focus more on what they are doing with their swings, they will notice that the number of times they hit the target increases proportionately.

Coaching Points

- One of the useful aspects of tee hitting is that coaches can carefully observe hitting mechanics while taking the shortcomings of the live pitch out of the equation.
- Roam among hitting stations to instruct players on mechanics while they hit.
- Do not allow players to take more than five or six swings without a break when they work on a tee. This number correlates to the number of pitches that a player normally sees in an at-bat.

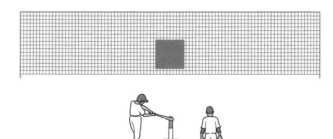

Over the Line

Age: *8 and older*   Skill Level: 🔵🔵

Introduction

One of the early inductees into Baseball's Hall of Fame, Wee Willie Keeler used to claim that he was successful because he would "hit 'em where they ain't." The following game takes that advice and combines it with a variation of a game that almost all sandlot ballplayers have played at one time or another. The game is fun for younger players and a good relaxer to introduce into practice occasionally with competitive high school teams. The objective of the game is to use good swing technique while trying to place the ball on a part of the field where the fielders "ain't." The game also encourages batters to hit up the middle of the field and helps train their swings to do so. An additional benefit of the game is that it challenges fielders to make sterling efforts to try to stop balls from getting by them. By employing the games approach strategies outlined in the introduction, coaches always have the option of making the game more demanding.

Equipment

Baseballs (regulation or softies), batting tee, eight cones

Setup

- ⊙ Divide the team in half; one team starts on offense, and the other starts on defense.
- ⊙ Place cones in two parallel lines about 60 to 75 feet (18 to 25 m) apart. The cones in each line should be 25 to 30 feet (8 to 10 m) from each other, and the first cones should be about 36 to 45 feet (11 to 15 m) from home plate. The area formed by the rectangle of the cones is considered fair territory.
- ⊙ If using a baseball field, the batting tee should be situated directly in front of home plate.
- ⊙ Position all defensive players in fair territory between the cones. Two to four players should be just in front of each of the lines made by the parallel cones.
- ⊙ Each line represents a base—the first line is a single, the second line is a double, etc.
- ⊙ One offensive player assumes a position at the tee. Other offensive players stand over to the side in a safe area.
- ⊙ The coach stands at the tee feeding balls and giving instruction.

Procedure

Play begins when the coach places a ball on the tee. The first hitter takes a swing and tries to hit the ball beyond the reach of the fielders within the area defined by the cones. If the ball is hit into fair territory, a hit is recorded for every line it crosses before the defense fields it. If the first line of defenders fails to field the ball cleanly, the batter is awarded a single even if the ball does not cross the first line. Players do not run the bases. Runs are scored by making consecutive hits and forcing in the imaginary runners.

Two strikes or foul balls constitute an out. Switch sides after three outs.

Defensive players attempt to field the batted ball cleanly before it crosses their line. After each out, rotate the lines of defenders. Return the ball to home plate.

Play as many innings as necessary. Coaches can adjust the boundaries and lines of the field to account for age or ability levels. The game can also be played using soft toss instead of a tee.

Coaching Points

◉ Caution players not to swing with an uppercut. Instead, they should work on hitting the top of the ball to produce a line-drive swing.

◉ Have players try to hit balls between fielders and up the middle.

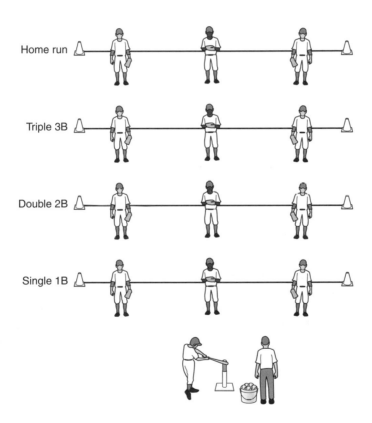

Flip It

Age: *10 and older*   Skill Level: *All*

Introduction

Besides having their teams hit off tees, most conscientious coaches incorporate some sort of soft toss or flip drills in their hitting stations. But as with tee hitting, most hitters don't really concentrate on what they are doing; they just whack at it! This game, similar to Target Hitting (page 134), forces awareness of not only the mechanics of the swing but also the results. Its goal is to get hitters to concentrate on hitting the ball on the sweet spot of the bat—on time and in time. In addition, by having players compete against one another, it generates more enthusiasm for the routine of soft toss.

Equipment

Baseballs, target net, clipboard, charts

Setup

- Divide players into groups of three.
- Set up flip stations along batting-cage or portable sock hitting nets.
- Place a dozen baseballs at each station.
- Have a clipboard and pencils available at the station.

Procedure

Flip stations can be set up along fencing, at sock nets, outside a batting tunnel net, along a fence, and so on. (If stations are used near fencing, use only rag balls or Wiffle balls to avoid damaging the fencing.) Coaches should hang targets on the netting or use paint or tape to mark target areas. Targets can be any dimension that a coach deems suitable for a particular age group or skill level. The targets can be circular, rectangular, or square. The key is that they should not be too large and should provide an area within which players are trying to hit the ball. An archery target might work well. A clipboard and chart that includes each player's name should be kept at the flip station. Alternatively, players could carry the chart with them from station to station. Simple charts with boxes for each day of the week and each hitting station—flip toss, tees, live, top-hand tee swings, and so on—would be sufficient. One player is the feeder, one is the hitter, and one charts each swing.

The feeder must be on one knee about 5 feet (1.5 m) to the side and to the front of the hitter. Play begins when the feeder tosses the first ball and the batter swings. The recorder marks the result, and the next ball is fed. A scoring system can be developed that awards points for hitting the target, coming close, and so forth. After five swings, which approximate an at-bat, players should rotate positions and begin again. Charts should be tallied daily, and scores should be posted in a prominent place to provide incentive for improvement. Occasionally, rewards should be given to leaders in categories or to players who improve the most from week to week.

Coaching Points

- The most important role in this game belongs to the player who is tossing the ball. Having the feeder on a knee forces him to become more of a participant.
- Make sure that the tossers flip the ball on a line and not on a looping arc. The toss should approximate a live pitch trajectory.
- Coaches should pay close attention to the hitter's load–stride–swing progression here, making sure that batters don't rush their mechanics.
- Limiting the amount of time spent at the station keeps the game lively. Normally 10 minutes is enough.

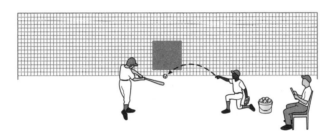

6.4 — Three-Man Bunting

Age: *12 and older*   **Skill Level:**

Introduction

Because of the importance of bunting—witness the lackluster efforts of professional players—a team can never practice bunting too much. A game that functions well in a gymnasium or in a confined outdoor space is Three-Man Bunting. Indoors, it provides another station to occupy players when space for hitting stations is limited. Playing the game regularly provides players with valuable knowledge of their strike zone, but more important, helps them develop a sense of how to maneuver the bat to direct the bunted ball where it needs to go.

Equipment

Baseballs, Wiffle balls, or rag balls; bats; throw-down home plate; fielder's gloves

Setup

- Divide players into groups of four.
- One player bunts, one pitches, one catches, and one fields.
- Use the throw-down home plate to mark the batting area.

Procedure

Before starting, tell players the rotation that they should follow. After a ball is bunted, the pitcher runs in and becomes the catcher. The bunter, after hitting a ball safely, takes three or four hard running steps up the line, picks up his glove, and replaces the fielder. The catcher tosses his glove about 10 feet (3 m) away from home along an imaginary first-base line, picks up a bat, and becomes the next bunter. The fielder fields the ball and moves into the pitcher's position to throw the next pitch. This rotation should be sharp and crisp. Players should be hustling continually.

The pitcher stands about 30 feet (10 m) from the bunter and throws medium-speed fastballs. (Indoors or with rag or Wiffle balls, the pitcher should be closer.) The fielder should stand in the direction that the coach wants the ball to be bunted. For example, if a runner is on first base, balls should be bunted toward the first baseman for maximum efficiency. In this game then, the fielder stands somewhere to the left of the pitcher about the same distance away from the batter. Batters should be trying to bunt the ball at the fielder.

Batters should bunt only strikes. When the ball is bunted fair, the batter should start running, pick up his glove, and then replace the fielder.

Time the station. Give players 10 minutes before ending the game and moving to another station. The player with the most balls bunted directly at the fielder is the winner. Coaches should reward winners in some fashion to accentuate the importance of the skill. Keep a daily record if possible. During the game, on the coach's command, fielders should shift positions to simulate different areas on the field for the bunters to aim at—left side of the infield, right side of the infield, closer to the foul lines, and so on. Balls hit back to the pitcher obviously do not count as successful bunts.

Coaching Point

● Focus on the bunting techniques of the players. Are they bending their back knees? Is the barrel of the bat out in front of the plate? Are the hands relaxed?

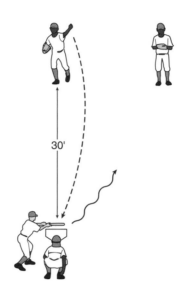

6.5

Wastebasket Bunting

Age: *10 and older*   **Skill Level:** *All*

Introduction

Many players are poor bunters because they fail to put enough focus and concentration into the act. This game gives players a visual focal point and creates a fun learning environment. It teaches players to bunt the ball in a narrow corridor near the foul lines, away from the pitcher's mound. It can help develop skill in both sacrifice bunting and drag bunting. As before, coaches should instruct and rigorously drill players in the mechanics of the various types of bunting before playing.

Equipment

Baseballs, bats, two small wastebaskets, sock net, field liner or cones

Setup

○ Divide the squad into two teams. One team is at bat, and the other is in the field.

○ The coach is the pitcher (the distance may be shortened).

○ Place the two wastebaskets, one near each foul line, about 20 feet (6 m) from home plate and about 2 feet (60 cm) inside the line.

○ Use a sock net as the catcher.

○ Mark a no-hit zone with field liner or use cones to delineate the area.

Procedure

The defensive team takes up positions anywhere on the infield behind the wastebaskets. Defensive players serve only as shaggers for the pitcher. The team at bat forms a line in foul territory near the plate. The first person in line becomes the batter and takes his stance within the batter's box. The coach throws a pitch. The batter bunts, trying to bunt the ball into either of the wastebaskets. Each bunt receives a score depending on a prearranged scoring scale. The following is a sample scoring rubric:

○ Ball bunted in the bucket—five points

○ Ball bunted within 1 foot (30 cm) of either side of the barrel—four points

○ Ball bunted within 5 feet (1.5 m) of the fair side of the barrel—three points

○ Ball fouled off—minus one point

○ Ball bunted in the no-no zone directly at the pitcher—minus five points

If a player misses a pitch, fouls one off, takes a called strike, or tries to bunt a pitch that is not a strike, his turn is over and he goes to the end of the line. After each player has had one turn to bunt, the teams switch positions and the team in the field gets its chance to bunt. Game length is three innings. The team with the most points wins. Players love to argue about scoring when bunts end up in gray areas, but coaches should remind them that the judgment of the coach is final!

Having batters attempt only sacrifice bunts in one inning or perform only drag bunts the next creates additional complexity. Challenges can also be added by calling out various situations before a pitch. For example, if the coach calls, "Runner at first base" in a sacrifice situation, the batter must bunt the ball down the first-base line to receive points. Offer additional points for bunts that were properly executed according to the situation.

Coaches should keep individual and team scores, posting them often to motivate the players.

Coaching Points

- ◉ Closely monitor bunting mechanics.
- ◉ Especially watch the back knee to make sure that it bends sufficiently to get the batter low enough to bunt properly.

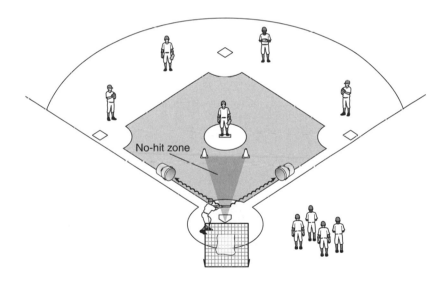

6.6

Four-Corner Bunting

Age: *12 and older*   **Skill Level:** ●●●●

Introduction

All coaches agree that bunting is an integral part of the game, but the only daily practice that players typically get in the skill is laying down two balls before taking batting practice in the cage. The following game gives players practice in all the bunting skills that they need to master and provides a competitive, gamelike atmosphere. Before playing the game, coaches should instruct and rigorously drill players in the mechanics of the various types of bunting.

Equipment

Baseballs, bats, bases

Setup

- Divide the squad into four equal groups and place one group at each of the bases including home plate. For more authenticity, the bases may be replaced by throwdown rubber home plates if they are available.
- Have balls and bats available at each base.
- One coach or player acts as a pitcher at each base about 30 feet (10 m) from the base.

Procedure

Before beginning play, designate each of the bases for a particular type of bunt. One way to do this is to have home plate the sacrifice bunt station, first base for drag bunts, second base for push bunts, and third base for the suicide squeeze station.

One batter in each group steps up to the plate and takes his normal batting stance. The pitcher at each base then throws a pitch, and the batter reacts as he might for the type of bunt required. For example, if the bunt called for at a station is a sacrifice, the batter may get into bunt position before the pitcher begins his motion. If a drag bunt is required, the batter must wait until the pitcher is well along in the motion before showing bunt.

Pitchers must throw only fastballs for the purpose of this game, but because they are close to the hitters, they should not throw harder than about 60 percent speed. Players waiting their turns to bunt should stand far enough away from the batter to avoid being hit by foul balls. After the batter bunts a ball, he sprints toward the next station. To avoid injury, runners should run only three-fourths of the way to the next base and then assume a position at the end of the line at the new station. If the batter fouls off the bunt or misses, he must go to the end of the line at his station and wait for another turn.

Coaches can implement other rules that send players to the end of the line. For example, attempting to bunt a nonstrike in a sacrifice situation requires the player to go to the end of the line. The first player who completes all four stations twice wins the game. Another way to score is to consider each group at a station a team. Then the first team that completes all four stations is declared the winner. Incentives for winning should be developed. If players are used as pitchers, devise a substitution plan so that they can take part in the game.

Coaching Points

- Remind players to bunt only strikes, especially in a sacrifice situation.
- Caution players not to leave the batter's box too early. They should make sure that the ball is on the ground before moving. The exception, of course, is the drag bunt, when players are almost running as they bunt.
- Make certain that players are not swinging the bat forward as they bunt. They must "catch" the ball with their bats.

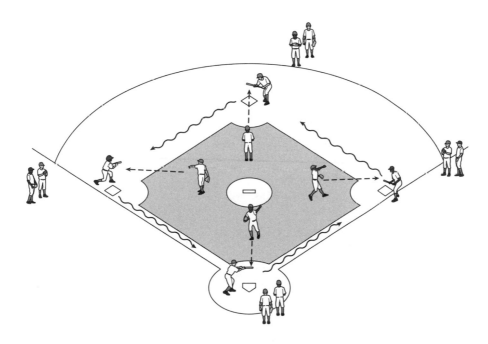

Hit the Target

Age: *12 and older*   **Skill Level:** 🞉🞉🞉🞉

Introduction

Often, when players do batting drills from a tee or with soft toss, they aren't really concerned with where the ball goes after they hit it; they just try to make contact. This game requires players to focus on what they are doing with the bat, where they are making contact, and what their hands are doing during the swing. Ten minutes of practice time should be allotted for the game. Players should play the game in groups of three.

Equipment

Baseballs, batting tee, throw-down home plate, target net

Setup

- Use tape or paint to mark a target area on the net. The target should be approximately 2 feet (.6 m) from the ground at the bottom, 6 feet (1.8 m) from the ground at the top and about 4 feet (1.2 m) wide.
- Place a tee 5 feet (1.5 m) from the target or net. (The tee should be moved to appropriate position in relation to home plate to simulate inside and outside pitches and pitches down the middle of the plate, depending on the skill being worked on.)
- Both the tee and the plate need to be moved in relation to the target when the hitting location is changed (for example, from an inside pitch to an outside pitch).
- One player hits, one player stands off to the side of the tee and places balls from the bucket on to the tee, and the third player gathers all the balls after each round and returns them to the bucket.
- Players rotate after every five swings.

Procedure

Players should each take three rounds of hitting in the time allotted. Round 1 focuses on the inside pitch. Place the tee about 12 inches (30 cm) in front of the inside corner of the plate (left side for a right-handed batter). Position the tee and the plate so that the center of the target is simulating the left-field side of the diamond from the foul line to the position normally occupied by the shortstop. Round 2 simulates a pitch down the middle. Move the tee to a point 6 inches (15 cm) in front of the plate and in the middle. Position the tee and the plate so that the center of the target would be the pitcher's mound. Round 3 simulates an outside pitch or breaking ball. Place the tee so that it sits on the outside corner of the front of the plate. The tee and the plate should be aligned with the target so that the center of the target is simulating the right-field side of the diamond from the foul line to the position normally occupied by the second baseman. Players hit five balls per round.

Scoring: Give a point for each ball hit off the tee into the target area. Scoring could be modified to deduct points for balls hit significantly above the top of the target (that is, popups).

Coaching Points

- Pay close attention to the position of the hands at contact. Rolling over the wrists too soon usually results in balls driven directly into the ground or pulled foul.
- Watch hip rotation.
- Make certain that hitters keep their hands inside the ball.
- As with other hitting stations, never allow players to take more than five swings without resting for a while. A set of five swings accurately reflects a typical at-bat in a game.

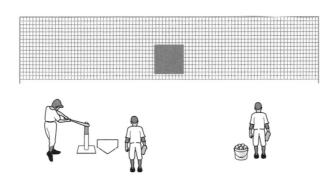

Pepper

Age: *12 and older*   **Skill Level:** 🔵🔵🔵🔵

Introduction

Maybe it started when they began hanging "No pepper" signs in every major league park, but whatever the reason, the age-old game of pepper has been in decline ever since, replaced by flip, its poor substitute. As a result, scores of young players can't watch their heroes in the big leagues playing a warm-up game of pepper on the sidelines before a game. And perhaps there is a connection between the decline of pepper and the lackluster fielding mechanics of current players. Despite recent trends, however, baseball players should still play pepper. Besides being an excellent game to train eye–hand coordination—players can actually see the ball hit the bat—pepper gives fielders many opportunities to develop quicker hands. Because they have to hit the ball to a limited area, batters learn how to use the bat to direct the ball where they want it hit. To be of benefit, however, the game must be played quickly. After all, it's called pepper, not molasses!

Equipment

Baseballs

Setup

- Divide players into groups of five or six.
- One player bats, and the others fields.
- Use a throw-down home plate to mark the batting area.
- The game can be played on any area of a field. (Use a fence or the outside of a batting tunnel as a backstop if possible.)

Procedure

The batter stands near home plate holding his bat in a choked-up position so that he has better bat control. The fielders, in good fielding position, should form a loose semicircle about 20 feet (6 m) from the batter. They should be about 3 feet (1 m) apart. Play begins when one of the fielders throws a pitch to the batter at half-speed. The batter tries to hit moderately hard ground balls or line drives back at the fielders. The player who fields the batted ball then throws another pitch to the batter at half-speed. The batter hits the ball back. Play continues in this fashion until the batter swings and misses or hits a popup. When this happens, the batter loses his turn and becomes a fielder. The fielder farthest left in the line (from the batter's perspective) becomes the next hitter and bats until he misses or pops up. The batter's turn also ends if he hits the ball too far outside the ends of the fielding line.

Fielders must throw strikes. If they fail to do so, they must rotate to the end of the line. In addition, if a fielder makes an error, he rotates to the end of the line. If a pitch is out of the strike zone and the batter does not swing at it, the batter returns the ball to one of the fielders in line for another pitch.

Players can keep their own score. They should keep track of the number of balls hit consecutively without a miss or a popup. The winner could be the batter who had the longest uninterrupted string. Coaches can devise other scoring methods to determine winners. Players hate to make mistakes in this game. Everyone's goal is to be the batter and to bat for as long as possible, so players will focus on being quick with their hands. Fielders will even attempt to steal balls away from players on their left or right because they want to be able to throw the ball and perhaps cause the batter to mishit it.

Coaching Points

- Caution the fielders that they must throw strikes. If they don't, they must rotate to the end of the line.
- Tell fielders that when they make an error, they must rotate to the end of the line.
- Remind fielders that after throwing the ball they must quickly assume fielding position.
- Make certain that players take the game seriously. They must pitch the ball with some mustard on it, but at the same time they can't fire the ball at 75 miles per hour (120 km/h).
- Keep players focused.

6.9 — **Read the Pitch** —

Age: *12 and older*   **Skill Level:** 🥎🥎🥎🥎

Introduction

See the ball; hit the ball. This maxim has been a mantra for hitting coaches probably since hitting was deemed important enough to be called a science. But as any coach can testify, this is easier said than done. Although the objective of that saying—to get players to relax, not think, and just hit the ball—is commendable, its execution is often just out of reach. To become better hitters, players must be able to read the ball early in the pitcher's release, process this information, and make a swing based on it. The following game gives hitters practice in pitch recognition while at the same time giving pitchers work in throwing to targets. The goals of the game are to allow hitters to recognize the path that breaking pitches take as opposed to the path of fastballs and changeups and to give them practice in reading the spin of the ball. These skills in turn should help players develop a better hitting eye and theoretically become smarter, better hitters.

Equipment

Batting tunnel, baseballs, protective net, clipboard, charts, batting tee (optional)

Setup

- Pair up hitters and use the batting tunnel as one of daily hitting stations.
- A pitcher is on the mound in the tunnel.
- A coach is stationed near the pitcher in back of the tunnel.
- Place a large field protection screen in the tunnel halfway from pitcher's mound to home plate. The screen should be at least 7 feet (2 m) high.
- With athletic tape or something more permanent, mark a strike zone on the protective net about 5 inches (12.5 cm) higher than it would be if marked at home plate (this adjustment allows for the 10-inch (25 cm) height difference between the pitcher's mound and home plate).

Procedure

In this game, pitchers throw to the target on the protective net. The ball will not pass the hitter. The first batter takes his position in the batter's box. The coach tells the pitcher what pitch to throw to which location in the strike zone. The pitcher throws the pitch at the target on the screen. When the ball is released the hitter calls the type of pitch and its location, for example, fastball up, fastball in, curve away, and so on.

When they first begin playing the game, batters should just try to call the type of pitch. As they become more proficient at identifying the type, batters should also call the location—up or down, in or out. Batters must simulate a swing or take a pitch on every throw in this game.

To complicate the game, the coach can place a tee in front of the hitter and require the hitter to hit the ball off the tee as the pitch reaches the halfway point. Batters must load, stride, and swing while making the call. The on-deck hitter keeps a chart, making note of the call of the hitter on each pitch. Repeat 10 times.

The coach also notes the pitcher's throws and keeps track on a pitching chart. If a pitch gets away from the pitcher—for example, the pitcher wants to throw low and away but actually throws high—the coach should make note and coach the pitcher for better results.

After each round, the pitching and hitting charts should be compared. Batters are scored on the number of correct calls that they make. Results should be recorded and posted.

Coaching Points

- Make sure that batters are loading and swinging with good rhythm, not just going through the motions. In a game, batters have less than one second to recognize a pitch and swing.

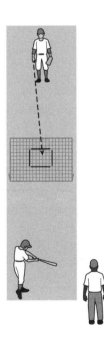

Short Toss

Age: *12 and older* **Skill Level:** ●●●●

Introduction

As a link between flip toss and live batting in the hitting continuum, short toss provides an opportunity for coaches to reproduce game conditions yet completely control the location of pitches. The goal of this game is to develop the hitter's focus on the release point and help develop the sense of timing of the swing in a fail-safe situation. Because the tosser is close to the plate, he can more easily throw the ball repeatedly to the same location to help the hitter work on weaknesses in his swing. The key for the coach is to toss the ball so that the batter has the same amount of reaction time as he does with a live pitch. After the coach has established a rhythm with the throws, he can easily change speeds by tossing either more lightly or more quickly. This technique enables the coach to keep the hitter honest yet help him develop timing. Because few pitches are wasted, batting practice with this game goes quickly and frees up more time for other skill development.

Equipment

L-screen, bucket of baseballs, clipboard, charts, catcher's gear

Setup

- Set the screen 10 to 12 feet (3 to 3.5 m) in front of home plate between the mound and the plate.
- Place a bucket of balls behind the screen.
- Divide the team into hitting groups of three or four.
- To control situations better, coaches may decide to do the tossing in this game.
- An assistant coach, parent, or manager should keep a tally of hitters' performances on a predesigned chart.

Procedure

This game can be used any day in place of normal batting practice. As with other games detailed here, a player should take only five or six swings at a time before a new hitter moves into the batter's box.

The first batter in a group assumes his position in the batter's box. The feeder, behind the screen, takes a ball out of the bucket, raises it up to the L throwing position, and flips it forward toward the hitter with a quick snap of the wrist. Batters should be instructed to begin their loading action when the tosser's hand reaches its highest point. After the appropriate number of swings, rotate batters and begin again. Batters should get three rounds before the next group comes in to hit.

A sample scoring system follows:

0 Missed swing
1 Foul tip, foul straight back, or foul at the dugout
2 Foul bunt, weak foul down the line, or popup anywhere
3 Sharp foul down the line or any high fly ball in the outfield
4 Weak fair ground ball or fair humpback liner
5 Fair bunt, hard ground ball, long fly, or line drive foul near the line
6 Line shot on the ground or in the air in fair territory

Establish specific and detailed qualifications for points to eliminate judgment calls by the scorekeeper. If an assistant coach is not available to do the scoring, coaches can involve parents in a positive way by appointing them to record the scores.

Coaching Points

- Vary the speed of the flip tosses so that players do not become too comfortable with their swing timing.
- Lob the ball slightly when replicating a breaking pitch.
- Make certain that players are getting into launch position and keeping their hands back.
- Throw bad pitches occasionally so that players can work on their strike zone recognition.

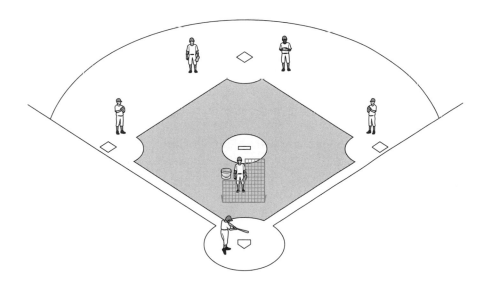

6.11 — **Right Side**

Age: *12 and older*   **Skill Level:** ●●●●

Introduction

One of the keys to the success of the hit-and-run is hitting the ball behind the runner. Most young players don't get enough repetitions to practice doing this. To be proficient in hitting behind the runner, batters need rehearsal in the skill. The following game gives players numerous opportunities to hit to right field and forces them to keep their hands inside the ball while focusing on lagging the barrel of the bat behind their hands with an inside-out swing.

Equipment

Baseballs, bats, cones, pitching machine (optional)

Setup

- Place a cone in the base line about 15 feet (5 m) on the third-base side of second base.
- Place another cone in center field in a direct line from home plate through the cone in the infield.
- A batter stands in the batter's box.
- A catcher is optional; a sock net can be used in place of a catcher.

Procedure

Use this game as part of normal batting practice. Players cycle through hitting stations and use this game for the live-hitting portion. If a pitching machine is used, set it so that it throws balls to the half of the plate on the right-field side. If a pitcher is used, a coach should pitch and throw the ball outside to a right-handed batter (inside to a left-hander).

Batters begin live batting practice with 20 points. Each ball hit to the right side of the cones counts as 1 point; each hit to the left counts as 4. Popups count as 2 points. Batters continue to hit until they accumulate 20 points.

Coaching Points

- Observe players' hitting techniques and instruct them accordingly.
- Watch to be certain the right-handed batters do not pull the front shoulder out.
- Make sure that hitters aren't "casting" the barrel of the bat. This common mechanical error works against hitting to right field.
- Tell left-handed batters to pull the ball by getting their hips through quickly.

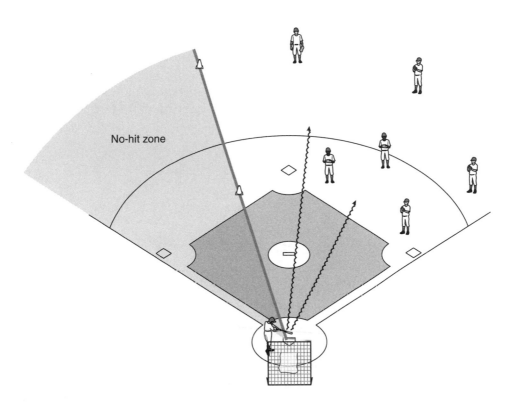

No-hit zone

Top Hand, Bottom Hand

Age: *12 and older*   Skill Level: ⚾⚾⚾⚾

Introduction

Another game that can be used in daily hitting stations to develop proper swing mechanics is Top Hand, Bottom Hand. The game is essentially the same as tee hitting except that the hitter can use only one arm. Isolating one arm forces the batter to concentrate on the role of each hand and arm in the swing. Some players roll their wrists over too early in the swing, which leads to weak ground ball swings. Others stay too stiff with the front arm and cast the bat. This station can help cure both of those swing ailments. The added dimension of the target gives immediate feedback to the hitter.

Equipment

Baseballs, batting tee, target net, clipboard, charts

Setup

- ⊙ Divide players into pairs.
- ⊙ Set up a tee along the batting cage or at a portable sock hitting net.
- ⊙ Place a dozen balls at the station.
- ⊙ Hang a target according to the skill being developed.
- ⊙ Have a clipboard and pencils available at the station.

Procedure

To begin, players should work on the bottom hand. They should assume a stance in proximity to the tee, holding the bat as they normally do when in their stance. They place the top hand under the armpit of the front arm and hold it there throughout the swing. Play begins when the feeder places a ball on the tee and the batter swings. After each swing, the feeder places another ball on the tee and the batter swings again. The feeder keeps track of results on a predesigned chart. Points can be given for balls hit into the target area or for hard-hit balls. After five swings, players rotate and change roles. Because the drill can be tiring, players should complete no more than two rounds with each hand.

For the second round, players again assume their stance, but this time they hold the bat only in the top hand (see figure). They place the bottom hand under the armpit of the top hand and hold it there. Because this swing is much more difficult, players should choke up on the bat considerably so that they don't have to force the swing.

Another way of doing this drill is to use any number of small wooden one-hand training bats on the market today, available online or in sporting goods stores.

Coaches should post the results and review them periodically to help players evaluate their progress and challenge them to succeed.

Coaching Points

- ◉ Watch that players are not sweeping the bat with the bottom hand but instead are taking the hand directly and firmly to the ball.
- ◉ Watch that players are not rolling their wrists too early, especially when isolating the top hand. Early wrist rolls lead to weak ground balls.
- ◉ Remind players that they should be able to self-correct their swings by observing where they hit balls in relation to the target and then making appropriate adjustments.

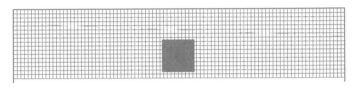

6.13 — **Triangle Hitting**

Age: *12 and older*   **Skill Level:** ◔◔◔◔

Introduction

Most players don't work enough on hitting to the opposite field. This important tactical skill is key to advancing runners, especially with the hit-and-run on. This game, which can be played in a confined space, helps players work on the inside-out swing necessary to the opposite-field approach. Although it was originally designed for use as an indoor batting station for inclement weather, the game can be played outdoors and can even become one of the stations that players use in their daily progression to live hitting. The objective of the game is to hit the ball to the right side (if a right-handed batter, or to the left side if left-handed) within the 45-degree angle triangle created by a pitcher, a batter, and a cone marking the right-field line as shown in the figure . A secondary goal, which might become the primary goal as players develop the skill, is to hit the ball hard on the ground.

Equipment

Container of Wiffle balls, throw-down home plate, cone

Setup

- Divide players into groups of three.
- One player bats, one player pitches, and one player fields.
- Use a throw-down home plate to mark the batting area.
- Place a cone 30 feet (10 m) from the batting area to mark the foul line.
- Use an open area of the field that will not interfere with live batting practice.

Procedure

The pitcher kneels on one knee 15 feet (5 m) from the batter and flips Wiffle balls into the strike zone. If the pitch is a ball, the batter should take. If the pitch is a strike, the batter must try to hit the ball to the opposite field between the cone marking the foul line and the pitcher. The fielder should react and try to field all balls hit into his area. Players take five to eight swings and then quickly rotate positions. The fielder moves to pitcher, the pitcher bats, and the batter becomes the fielder. If necessary, coaches can add additional players to reduce the time spent chasing balls. Indoors, this is not a problem, and the game functions well with only three players.

The pitcher must be consistent with the location of the flips. Most athletes should be able to throw strikes from 15 feet (5 m) without too much difficulty. After each flip, pitchers should duck their heads in case a ball is hit right back at them. Wiffle balls won't cause injuries, but they can sting for a while from that distance.

Because the distance between the batter and fielder is short, the game helps fielders work on their reactions to batted balls.

Score can be kept simply by keeping track of the number of balls hit into the triangular area and posting the results. Popups should not be counted as successful hits.

Coaching Points

- Observe that batters keep their hands inside the ball on their swings and that they extend their arms.
- Remind them to become conscious of the barrel of the bat lagging behind their hands.

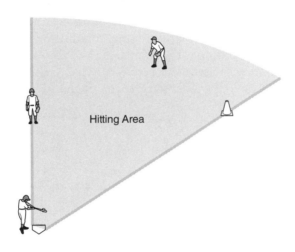

Hitting Area

Walk-Through

Age: *12 and older*   **Skill Level:** ●●●●

Introduction

Most hitting instruction moves along a hitting continuum from closed (static) to open (dynamic) drills. Dry swings and tee hitting by their nature are closed drills. The element of the live pitch is eliminated, and the focus is on the mechanics of the swing only, not judgment or timing. Flip toss and short-toss drills are more dynamic because the ball is in motion, so the batter must react to the ball as well as focus on mechanics. Live hitting and situation-type drills are completely dynamic because the hitter has to react to a live pitch under game conditions. This game bridges the gap between static and dynamic drills by injecting rhythm and timing into a static situation. Learned from the teaching of John Malee, Florida Marlins hitting coordinator, the drill combines the static nature of regular tee hitting with the dynamics of movement. It helps a player become more cognizant of the relationship between the hands and the lower body in the swing. In short, it helps build the inner sense of timing that all proficient hitters have.

Equipment

Baseballs, batting tee, target net, clipboard, charts

Setup

- Divide players into groups of three.
- Set up a station along the batting cage or at a portable sock hitting net.
- Place a dozen balls at the station. Have clipboard and pencil available.

Procedure

The setup for this game is similar to the setup for Target Hitting (page 134) with the following differences. One player hits, one player feeds balls on the tee, and the third player charts the results. As with other games in this chapter, a target should be used.

The batter sets up in a relaxed position about 3 feet (1 m) behind the tee. His chest should be perpendicular to its normal position in a hitting drill—the navel faces the target and the bat rests on the back shoulder. The feeder places a ball on the tee. Next, the batter takes a short step forward with his back foot (the right foot for a right-hander) while opening the foot parallel to the target at the same time. Then, the batter takes a stride step with the lead foot while simultaneously bringing the hands back into launch position. After the stride step, the hands should be in their loaded position and the batter should swing at the ball as in any tee drill. The additional player keeps the chart and records the location and direction of the ball in regard to the target. At first, players may have to experiment with their starting location in relationship to the tee so that the bat meets the ball at the proper contact position. After the hitters become proficient, the tee can be shifted to replicate not only pitches down the middle but also inside and outside pitches. The tee should be shifted so that its angle to the target is correct for the type of swing being practiced.

As with all hitting games, scores should be kept and posted to provide a competitive daily atmosphere.

Coaching Points

- Make certain that players stay fluid throughout this game. A tendency with young players is to become robotic with their movements.
- Remind players that rhythm is extremely important and that they must be loose. They should try to perform in one continuous rhythmic motion, not 1, then 2, then 3.
- Have players bring the front knee to the back knee while taking the stride step. This action helps them glide to the ball rather than jump to it.
- Emphasize the correct path of the bat during the swing. Watch for players who cast the bat with the barrel first.
- When the hands move into launch position, have players bring the bat back with the top hand, not the bottom hand. Using the bottom hand promotes wrapping of the bat and a long swing.
- Most important, make sure that they stride *to* swing, not stride and swing at the same time.

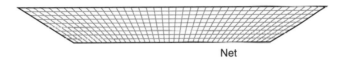

Net

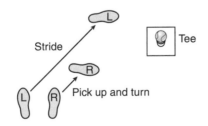

Timing Sticks

Age: *12 and older*   **Skill Level:** 🟡🟡🟡🟡🟡

Introduction

Hall of Fame lefty Warren Spahn once said, "Hitting is timing and pitching is destroying timing." As a master of the latter, Spahn used a variety of pitches to keep hitters off balance, and he became the winningest left-hander in the history of the game. Because pitchers work daily to destroy batters' timing, batters who want success should be working just as diligently to develop a better sense of timing. One way to create better timing is first to destroy a batter's comfort zone and then help him create a new inner sense of timing. This can be accomplished by using bats, or hitting sticks, of various weights interchangeably. The inspiration for this particular game comes from Perry Husband of California, the owner of GuessWorks, but its genesis is found in the old-fashioned game of stickball. Besides developing timing, this game encourages hitting inside the ball, eye–hand coordination, and the ability to react to changes in speed and direction—all advantageous hitting traits.

Equipment

Three 48-inch (120 cm) sticks of various weights, several dozen XLR8 or similar foam-type balls or golf-size Wiffle balls, bucket

Setup

- The game is best played in a contained area such as a gym or smaller room.
- A coach acts as a soft-toss feeder.
- Players work in pairs so that they have time to rest between stages.

Procedure

To begin, coaches should first create the hitting sticks. The normal stick should be a regulation broomstick handle about 48 inches (120 cm) long. The extra length helps ensure that batters cannot cast the barrel of the bat at the ball first. They will have no success if they try to start the swing by casting the end of the bat to the ball first instead of the hands, especially when using the heavy stick.

For a light stick, coaches should cut a piece of plastic PVC tubing to a length of 48 inches (120 cm). The heavy bat can be built with a 4-foot length of steel conduit pipe with threaded ends. Fit caps to the ends. Place tape on all sticks to enable players to grip them more securely. Other materials can be used, but the basic principle is to create three bats that are significantly different in weight from one another.

The game begins with the batter taking his stance with the normal weight hit stick. The coach should be in soft-toss feeder position off to the side of the hitter and slightly in front. When the feeder's hand moves backward to initiate the toss, the batter should begin his swing with his loading action. The feeder tosses the ball, and the batter swings. If golf-sized Wiffle balls are used, eye–hand coordination becomes much more important than it is in regular soft toss. If XLR8 balls are used as recommended, eye–hand coordination plays an increased role but reacting to change of speeds becomes paramount.

After five or six swings, players should switch sticks and use the heavy stick. Repeat the process of soft toss for five or six more swings. Players then take the light stick and do the same. Finish the round with the normal bat. Switch batters and repeat the sequence twice. The on-deck batter should keep track of how many times the batter hits the ball fair with each stick (determine fair territory before starting). In the beginning, this simple way of scoring is sufficient because many players will initially miss the ball completely with the light or heavy sticks. As players develop their sense of inner timing and can more adequately discern the speed difference, the charts could reflect the increase in quality of the balls hit.

When played regularly, especially during the off-season or preseason, the game develops a superior sense of timing and rhythm and increased eye–hand coordination. Swinging each bat requires a different sense of body timing, the theory being that each time a batter changes timing, his body will improve that inner sense of timing that all great hitters have. Timing then becomes a subconscious, and therefore more reliable, skill.

Coaching Points

- Explain to players before they play the game that they will not be immediately successful.
- Always use a portable home plate to simulate game conditions.
- If possible, use XLR8 balls. They come in two styles that are differentiated by the density of the foam in the ball. Because of this difference, when the two types are thrown with the same motion, they move at different speeds, reproducing game conditions.
- Make sure that batters take full swings and don't merely lunge at the ball.
- Watch closely to ensure that they load and stride properly

Tape on handle   **Hitting stick**   48" long

6.16 ──────── Speed Stik ────────

Age: *12 and older*   **Skill Level:** ⚾⚾⚾⚾⚾

Introduction

When pro and college scouts evaluate young players, one of their prime considerations is bat speed. They know that speed equates to distance and that distance equals power. The following game, which employs the Speed Stik, develops quicker hands, leading to improved bat speed. The Speed Stik is a heavy metal training device that comes in two sizes for baseball, 42 and 36 inches (107 and 91 cm) in length, and features a built-in device that measures bat speed in miles per hour. Besides helping to develop bat speed, the game and the device are helpful for developing an inside-out, hands-inside-the-ball type of swing. The Speed Stik can be used at a daily hitting station, and the game takes only a short time to complete.

Equipment

Speed Stik, golf-sized Wiffle balls or soft foam-type balls, bucket, chart and clipboard, gym mat or similar piece of equipment

Setup

- ◎ Set up a station so that players hit into mat, thereby containing the balls in a small area.
- ◎ Players pair up; one swings, and the other records performance; or one hits into mat, and the other tosses.

Procedure

To begin play, the batter performs several swing exercises with the Speed Stik as explained in the product manual. The first is five continual nonstop swings from the player's dominant side. From the batting-stance position, players swing the bat from the back side to the follow-through position, shifting their weight accordingly with the swing. After they reach the follow-through position, the players reverse the swing back to the starting position in one continuous motion, sort of like a reverse slow-motion replay of the swing. After they are back at the starting point, they swing again and repeat the process five times. The next exercise is to perform the same drill with the nondominant side. Following that, players swing with one arm in the same fashion—first with their strong hand and then with their weak arm. Because of the weight and length of the Speed Stik, players need to start slowly and build up to full speed.

Players in each pair should keep daily charts of each other's performance. At the end of each stage—dominant swings, nondominant swings, one-arm swings, and so on—players should take the last swing with maximum speed. After taking the maximum swing, the speed should be recorded and the results should be posted regularly on a chart in the locker room. Using the Speed Stik or a similar device challenges players to improve their bat speed, which in turn should improve their hitting.

Enterprising coaches can devise hitting drills using foam or Wiffle balls to take advantage of the features of the Speed Stik. Use only soft foam-type balls or Wiffle balls if the Speed Stik is used for hitting. Anything heavier could damage the device.

Coaching Point

⊙ Coaches need to keep a close eye on swing mechanics when players are swinging for maximums. They will sometimes try to force their swings to increase the reading on the gauge of the Speed Stik. Eventually, players will learn by themselves that swinging harder does not equate to higher speed on the Speed Stik.

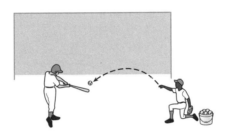

Take or Hit

Age: *12 and older*   **Skill Level:** 🥎🥎🥎🥎

Introduction

Many coaches have become prematurely gray watching their batters swing at pitches that are ankle high or over their heads. Although some of these swings result simply from players being fooled by good pitches, many of them occur because players have little concept of what constitutes a strike or a ball. When used as part of a daily hitting-station rotation, this game increases players' recognition of their personal strike zones and aids in the swing-or-take decision-making process.

Equipment

Tennis or Wiffle balls, throw-down home plate, pitching L-screen, batting tunnel

Setup

- Divide players into groups of three.
- One player bats, one pitches, and one catches and keeps score.
- Play the game in the batting tunnel or other confined area to minimize ball chasing.

Procedure

If using tennis balls, the pitcher can set up about 30 feet (10 m) from the plate. If Wiffle balls are used, the distance can be shorter. A pitching L-screen should be used for safety.

The batter assumes position in the batter's box. The pitcher throws a pitch to the batter. If the pitch is a strike, the batter should swing. If the pitch is a ball, the batter must take. The catcher calls balls and strikes. Batters receive points for taking balls and swinging at strikes. Points are deducted for swinging at balls and taking strikes. The catcher or a manager assigned to the station can keep score.

The pitcher should mix up pitches, throwing some low, some high, some inside, and some outside. He should even throw some at the hitters so that they can practice turning the shoulder in when being hit by a pitch.

Coaching Points

- Watch that players load properly on each pitch.
- Condition players to think that every pitch is going to be a strike and to take an aggressive mental approach to hitting. If they look only to take a pitch, they will never be able to catch up to the ball should they decide to hit.
- Remind them that if they are always ready to hit, they can easily transition into taking the pitch by simply relaxing and rotating inward.

CHAPTER
7

SITUATIONAL GAMES

Pickle

Age: *10 and older*   **Skill Level:**

Introduction

Former Tigers pitching star Earl Wilson once defined baseball as "simply a nervous breakdown divided into nine innings." Perhaps nothing in baseball brings a coach closer to the asylum than watching his team catch a runner between bases and then botch the ensuing rundown. Pickle is a throwback to the street ball game that many played as kids, called pickle in the middle—at least that is what it was called in Milwaukee. Whenever three kids with a ball and time on their hands congregated, one of them was the runner in the middle while the other two threw the ball back and forth trying to tag him out between the two cars that served as bases. Today, with all the fancy training devices used to teach the techniques of baseball, the simple technique of how to implement a rundown often becomes lost in the shuffle. Properly executing a rundown, or getting out of one, is a key tactic for any successful baseball team. This game helps players understand the main objectives of a rundown—tagging the runner out in as few throws as possible or making sure that the runner doesn't advance to the next base. Before playing the game, however, coaches should instruct their players in the techniques that they want them to use during rundowns—how to run after a caught runner, when to throw the ball, which direction to go after throwing, and so forth.

Equipment

Bases, baseballs, helmets

Setup

- Divide the team into two groups of equal numbers.
- One group will be base runners, and the other will be defensive players.
- Use only the baseline between any two of the bases.
- Coach observes and comments from the infield.

Procedure

The group that will be serving as base runners stands out of the way in foul territory near first base. One runner, wearing a helmet, takes a primary lead position about 15 feet (5 m) from first base and faces home plate. (With youth teams on a smaller field, adjust this distance.) One of the defensive players stands on first base awaiting a throw from second base. Another defensive player, with a ball in his hand, stands in the base line between first and second, a few feet inside second base. The other defensive players are divided equally into lines behind first base and second base.

Play begins when the player with the ball throws it to his teammate at first. When the runner hears the ball hit the glove, he is picked off and must try to advance to the next base or escape the rundown. Following the techniques taught by the coach, the defensive players try to tag the runner or, failing in that, force the runner back to the original base. After a defensive player has thrown the ball, he follows the ball and rotates to the end of the line opposite where he started. Another fielder in line takes his place. Players rotate in this fashion until the out is made or the runner reaches a base. The next runner in line takes a leadoff, and play continues. After each runner runs twice, teams switch roles; defenders become runners, and runners become defenders. To accommodate more players, a second line could be set up between third base and home plate.

The defense earns points for making outs, and the runners earn points for getting out of the pickle. Coaches can invent their own scoring system giving priority to making fewer throws.

Practicing with this game at least once a week helps coaches avoid gray hairs!

Coaching Points

- Make sure that the fielder receiving the first throw does not step forward to catch it. This gives an unfair advantage to the defense.
- In addition, see that the runner keeps his head forward and doesn't peek to anticipate that the fielder will catch the ball. This gives him an unfair advantage.
- Instruct defenders that they should limit arm fakes.
- Teach defenders to run hard at the picked-off runner if they see his face. Tell them to throw the ball to the receiving defender if they see the back of the player's helmet.

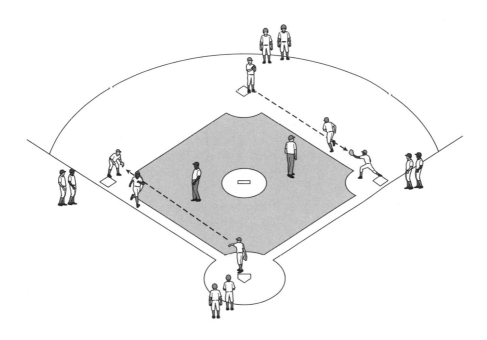

0-2 Breaking Ball

Age: *12 and older*   **Skill Level:** 🏐🏐🏐🏐

Introduction

Pitchers are often advised to throw waste pitches when ahead of the batter. Another leading cause of premature graying of a coach's hair is the 0-2 pitch that is too good and left hanging for a batter to smash somewhere. But can the pitcher really be blamed for hanging an 0-2 pitch if he doesn't get to practice it in real-time situations? This game serves three purposes: It gives pitchers an opportunity to throw the 0-2 strikeout pitch as well as hold runners; it gives catchers practice blocking curveballs; and it allows runners to work on extending their leads at first and automatically stealing second on balls in the dirt.

Equipment

Baseball, catcher's gear, bases

Setup

- A catcher is in full gear.
- A batter is in the batter's box. The batter does not swing but merely stands in the box.
- Fielders are at first base and second base.
- A line of runners is at first base.

Procedure

The catcher assumes receiving position behind the plate. The runner on first takes a primary lead. The batter stands in either batter's box. The pitcher may try to pick the runner at first base or throw home. Every pitch must be a breaking ball out of the strike zone. Any time the ball hits the dirt, the runner must try to steal second base. If the ball is not in the dirt, runners must return to the base. If the runner misreads the ball, the catcher may try to pick off the runner returning to the base. If the runner does not run on a ball in the dirt, he is out. The catcher may throw to first or second. After each pickoff or steal attempt, the next runner in line steps in. Switch pitchers and catchers occasionally.

   Keep a record of the catcher's blocking and throwing. Score two points for every runner thrown out at first or second base. For a successful steal, deduct two points. Give two points to the pitcher for a successful breaking ball out of the strike zone. Deduct points for pitches that are too close to being strikes.

Coaching Points

- Make sure that the catcher does not try to catch the balls in the dirt. The catcher's hands should try to beat his knees to the ground.

- Teach catchers to soften their upper bodies and lean their shoulders forward when blocking to try to keep the ball in front of them.

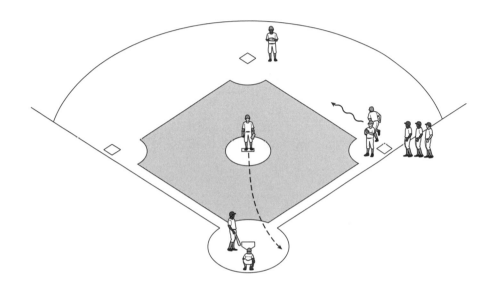

Advancing From Second

Age: *12 and older*   **Skill Level:** 🌑🌑🌑🌑

Introduction

More games are lost because of poor baserunning decisions than because of errors. This game helps players improve their ability to make split-second judgments about when to advance from second on a batted ball, when to retreat back to the base to tag, and when to hesitate and watch the play before making a decision. An added component is that it rewards aggressive play. It also gives defensive players game-speed practice at fielding ground balls and fly balls, making quick decisions on throws, and using cutoffs and relays. The game takes about 15 minutes to play and involves the entire team and a coach or fungo hitter. Try to play once a week early in the season.

Equipment

Five or six baseballs, fungo bat, bases

Setup

- Runners stand in a line near second base.
- Fielders are stationed at third base, shortstop, left field, center field, right field, and catcher.
- Divide the team into squads of three or four runners according to their running speed.
- Rotate runners and fielders if necessary.

Procedure

The game begins with one of the runners at second base taking a 15-foot (5 m) primary lead off the base. When the coach or fungo hitter tosses the ball in the air before hitting it, the runner should take a secondary lead. When the ball is hit, the runner reacts to the ball. The coach should hit ground balls, line drives, and fly balls at varying speeds at, in front of, and behind the runner. The runner should react to the speed and location of the batted ball, holding on ground balls hit in front of him and advancing on balls hit behind him. On balls hit directly at the runner, he must make a split-second judgment about whether to go or hold. On fly balls, the runner needs to judge whether to tag and advance or go halfway. On balls hit to the outfield, the runner has the option of trying to advance home. Again, he must make a good judgment. On all throws to the bases, no sliding is allowed. If a ball beats a runner to the base, the runner is out.

After each runner has two live attempts, place three more runners at second base. Rotate players in the field.

Scoring: Runners are scored on their first reaction and their decision making. The coach is the sole judge. The runners play against the ball and the defense. Coaches can devise a point system to reward aggressiveness and penalize bad judgment and conservative baserunning. Reward the team with the most points.

Coaching Points

● This game provides excellent opportunities for coaches to focus play. Teach players how to read the ball off the fungo bat and make a judgment based on the initial flight of the ball.

● Use this as an opportunity to teach proper secondary lead technique.

7.4 ——— **Cat and Mouse** ———

Age: *12 and older*   **Skill Level:** 🔵🔵🔵🔵

Introduction

When teams are aggressive on the bases, they compel a defense to be wary and often force them into mistakes. Teams have to be prepared to handle the challenges that a running game presents, and aggressive teams must continually hone their baserunning skills to keep their edge. This game prepares pitchers to be better at holding runners by giving them real-time practice with their pickoff moves and deliveries. It gives catchers practice on their pickoffs and throws to second base. And it gives runners chances to work on reading and getting good jumps on pitchers.

Equipment

Baseballs

Setup

- A batter is in the batter's box.
- Pitchers form a line near the mound.
- Runners with helmets stand in a line outside first base.
- One or two infielders take a position at second base.

Procedure

The first pitcher in line assumes a stretch position on the rubber, takes his sign, and then can either pick at first base or throw a pitch. The first runner takes a primary lead at first. If the pitcher throws home, the runner steals or takes a secondary lead. If the runner goes, the catcher throws to second base on the steal. To avoid injuries, no sliding is allowed. If the throw beats the runner to the base, the runner is out. If the runner takes too big a secondary lead, the catcher should try to pick him off first.

The runner must steal on one of the first three pitches during his time on the base. After each attempted steal, a new runner assumes a primary lead at first base.

The batter in the box should alternate between the right-hand and left-hand box to create gamelike conditions. The batter does not swing at any pitch. If the pitcher throws home, the first baseman must come off the base and get into ready fielding position. A coach could stand at third base and practice giving signs to the runners at first.

For scoring, the defensive team gets two points for every successful stop; the running team gets one point for each steal. This game can be extremely competitive if the stakes are high enough. Give incentives for winning.

Coaching Points

- Make certain that pitchers vary their moves to first base.
- Teach pitchers to have a slow, poor move and a quick, good move.
- Watch to be sure that they don't always throw with the same timing or rhythm.
- Work with runners to read pitchers' motions and get good jumps when stealing.

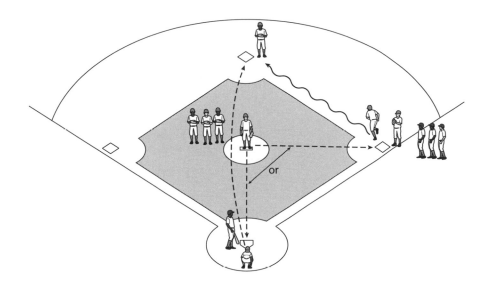

7.5 | Contact

Age: *12 and older*　**Skill Level:** 🔵🔵🔵🔵

Introduction

A runner can score from third base in nine ways—as opposed to only one from second.

1. Base hit
2. Sacrifice fly
3. Error
4. Balk
5. Wild pitch
6. Passed ball
7. Steal
8. Ground ball out
9. Squeeze bunt

Considering this, a major tactical objective at any level of baseball is to get runners to third base. From there, players can score on sacrifice flies, balks, wild pitches, and infield ground balls. This game helps players develop their baseball sense—the subconscious aptitude needed to make split-second decisions—about whether to go or stay on a ground ball. Coaches should prep players so that they are ready to read the play as it develops and apply the knowledge that they have gained in pregame or during the season. For example, to be able to score consistently on ground balls, players have to be aware of how hard or soft the field is, how the grass affects the bounce of the ball, how quick the third baseman is, where he is playing, how strong his arm is, and more. Playing this game trains players to react to a wide range of possibilities.

Equipment

Bases, bucket of baseballs, helmets, clipboard, charts

Setup

- A line of runners stands in foul territory near third base.
- Defensive players take positions at third base, second base, pitcher, and catcher.
- A coach with a fungo bat and bucket of balls is at home plate.
- A manager, player, or another coach keeps track of results on a chart.

Procedure

The first player in line takes a primary lead at third base. The pitcher comes to a set position and throws home. As the catcher receives the ball, the coach hits a ground ball fungo toward the third-base side of the infield, the second-base side, or directly back to the pitcher. Depending on where the ball is hit, the runner holds his lead, retreats to the base, or sprints home. If he runs home, the runner should run only three-fourths of the way down the line and then peel off and return to the end of the line. After each ground ball, the next person in line takes a primary lead at third base.

Coaches can score this game by giving either positive or negative marks to each player depending on his immediate reaction to the ball. Results can be posted and kept during the season. Here are some scoring examples: If the ball is hit sharply right back at the third baseman, the runner should stay unless the contact play is on. If the runner breaks for home on this ball, he would get a negative mark. On balls that take high hops or are hit slowly, runners have to see what the ball is doing early and break for home. Runners should stay on balls hit directly to the pitcher. If they are fooled, they need to learn how to get into a rundown to let the other runner or runners advance. On balls hit to the second-base side, runners should go automatically.

To make the game more challenging, coaches can shift the third baseman around, sometimes having him playing in front of the base, sometimes behind it, and so on. A change in the third baseman's positioning should be a cue for the runner to alter his primary lead. Coaches can also incorporate the contact play into this game, training runners to anticipate the swing but also to read the line drive, stop, and return to the base.

Coaching Points

- Train players in the appropriate way to take primary and secondary leads at third base.
- Make sure that runners don't commit too early or react too late.
- Caution players to lead off in foul territory.

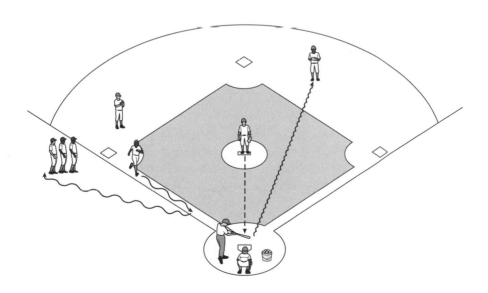

7.6 ——— **In the Hole** ———

Age: *12 and older*   **Skill Level:** 🔵🔵🔵🔵

Introduction

California coaching legend John Scolinos used to give a hilarious clinic presentation comparing the intelligence of a fly trapped in a car to that of one of his players who was having trouble hitting. The story never failed to produce laughter among the coaches in the audience, but at the same time it drummed home a solid truth about hitting. The fly, after slamming into the car windows a few times, would eventually use his instincts and find an escape route, but Scolinos' player was portrayed as stubbornly drilling into the same spot in the window, trying to force the window to move. The moral was simple: Hitters have to adjust their approaches and their swings to react to changing game situations. This batting-practice game requires players to react to changing counts and adjust their swings accordingly. Because the number of swings that they get in batting practice depends on their judgment, they focus more on pitch location.

Equipment

L-screen, bucket of baseballs

Setup

- The coach pitches from 35 to 40 feet (11 to 12 m) away to allow more accuracy.
- Insert the game into batting practice regularly.

Procedure

While players are taking their normal daily batting practice, with each batting-practice pitch thrown, the pitcher–coach should call out a pitch count, say 2-0, 3-1, or 0-2, and force the batter to react to the count. Batters should be selective in counts in their favor and defensive in counts in the pitcher's favor. For example, depending on the coach's approach to hitting, batters should maintain their normal stance when ahead in the count but widen the stance, choke up on the bat, and move closer to the plate when in the hole.

Also, when ahead, batters should be selective about the pitches at which they swing. On a 2-0 count, for instance, batters should be looking for fastballs from the middle of the plate in that they can drive hard. On a 3-1 count, batters should swing only at balls in their wheelhouse—the part of the strike zone that they like the best.

If the batter does not adjust appropriately to the count, the coach could subtract swings from the batter's total cuts for the day. If the coach throws a pitch low and outside on a 2-0 count and the batter swings, that swing would be considered a judgment error. On a 1-2 pitch, the batter should swing at any pitch close to the strike zone. If a batter makes three errors in judgment, he loses his turn and the next batter steps to the plate.

Because moving the ball around the strike zone is important in this game, a coach should pitch to maintain consistency. Moving the screen close helps ensure accuracy. Coaches can also throw curveballs in various counts to gauge the batter's ability to adjust.

Coaching Points

- Check to see that batters alter their batting stance according to the count. They should widen their stance and choke up on the bat in counts that favor the pitcher.

- Teach hitters to recognize curveballs up in the zone and swing at them, especially when ahead in the count.

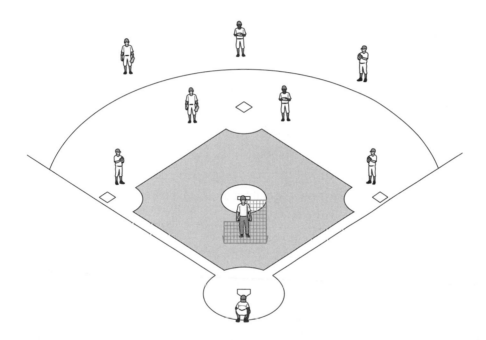

7.7 ━━━━━━━━ **Long Tee** ━━━━━━━━

Age: *12 and older*   Skill Level: 🟤🟤🟤🟤

Introduction

When players hit off tees, because they are only hitting a short distance, they usually don't really see the flight path of the ball, even when using a target. This game gives players a chance to see where they have hit the ball and concentrate on its trajectory. The game helps them work on hitting the sweet spot. When used occasionally as part of a hitting rotation, it enables players to get more of a feeling for what they are doing with the bat. And because the object of the game is to hit the ball in a certain direction, it compels the hitter to keep his hands inside the ball on the swing.

Equipment

Batting tees, cones, baseballs, gloves

Setup

- Use an area of the outfield away from other activity.
- Divide the team into groups of four.
- Set batting tees directly in line with one another about 150 feet (45 m) apart.
- Place cones 10 feet (3 m) to the right and left of the tees and parallel to them.

Procedure

Each group of four players works together in pairs. One player in each pair hits, and the other fields. Tees should be set up to replicate a pitch down the middle. Play begins when the feeder on team A places a ball on the tee. The batter hits the ball off the tee, trying to hit the ball toward team B while keeping it within the area defined by the cones. The fielder on team B, using good fielding technique, fields the ball and then places it on the tee in his area. The batter on team B hits the ball back to team A. Each hitter gets 10 swings, or play continues for as long as the coach deems necessary.

Devise a point system and have players keep score. Line drives or hard ground balls count three points, fly balls count one point, popups count zero points, and so on. Players compete in teams. Results should be kept, and scores should be posted.

In variations of the game, the tees could be adjusted to replicate inside or outside pitches. Batters would stand accordingly in relation to the tees. The area that they are hitting toward would have to be adjusted to reflect this variation. For example, if the tee is set for an outside pitch, the area toward which the ball is hit would have to be on a 45-degree angle from the tee, not directly across from it. This setup requires more space on the field, and additional safety precautions would have to be adopted.

Coaching Points

○ Watch to see that players' hands are staying inside the ball.

○ Vary the position of the tee frequently so that players can practice hitting inside and outside pitches as well as those down the middle.

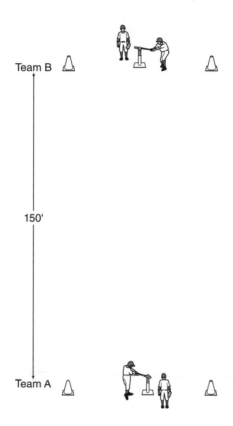

Team B

150'

Team A

7.8 — Overthrow

Age: *12 and older* **Skill Level:** ● ● ● ●

Introduction

Even when running to first base on a routine ground ball, aggressive players have to be aware of what is happening on the field and can't rely only on the first-base coach to tell them what to do. Besides teaching proper baserunning technique, this game helps players sharpen their recognition skills and make split-second judgments about advancing on overthrows.

Equipment

Baseball, bases, helmets

Setup

- Players line up in a single file at home plate.
- The coach, holding a ball in his hand, stands even with and 15 feet (5 m) to the foul side of first base.

Procedure

Players form a line behind home plate. On command, they sprint toward and through first base. When one player is 60 feet (18 m) from home plate, the next player in line begins running. After the runner crosses first, he must decelerate and immediately look to his right, trying to locate the ball. Occasionally, the coach should drop the ball to the ground as the runner is crossing first base. The runner, after seeing the ball on the ground, must react, change direction, and sprint for second base, depending on the location of the ball. The coach can toss the ball in various directions to simulate game situations. The runner should run two-thirds of the way to second and then return to the end of the line at home plate.

Scoring in this game is subjective. The coach should judge, based on the location of the ball and the ability of the runner, whether the runner made the correct decision. Points would be awarded for reacting correctly.

Coaching Points

● Make sure that runners stare straight ahead as they are running to first. If the runners watch the coach holding the ball, they would have an unfair advantage of knowing when to advance to second or when not to.

● Deduct points for runners who peek.

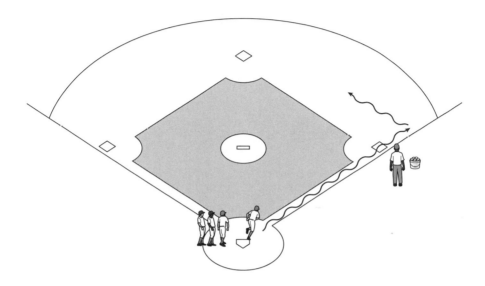

7.9 — Bobble and Go!

Age: *12 and older*   **Skill Level:** ●●●●

Introduction

Aggressive baserunning can add an exciting dimension to a team's offense. Knowing that another team is going to steal or try to take an extra base puts enormous pressure on a defense and often gets them out of the comfort zone. But teams cannot be aggressive unless coaches daily instill in them the self-confidence necessary to become gamblers and take chances. Playing this game enables players to be able to react quickly to mishandled plays and take the extra base automatically.

Equipment

Baseball, bases, helmets, fungo bat

Setup

- Two outfielders take positions in left field and center field.
- The remaining players form two lines at home plate.
- Place an additional first base approximately 20 feet (6 m) beyond the original first base and to the foul side so that it is symmetrical with the diamond.
- The coach stands to the left of home plate with a fungo.

Procedure

This game should be played as an extension of Overthrow (page 182), but the difference in approach is important. In this game, the runners will be running to first as if they had hit a ball through the infield.

Players form two lines at home plate. The two outfielders take ready positions in left and center field approximately 250 feet (75 m) from home plate. The coach tosses a ball in the air and hits balls to the outfield—either ground balls or line drives. When the first runner in each line hears the sound of the ball hitting the bat, he sprints toward first base. Runners in both lines must read the position of the ball and determine whether they should round first and hold or continue to second. If the ball is fielded cleanly, they should take a few hard steps toward second, pivot, and return to first. If the ball is in the gap between the outfielders, they should read the cues given—position of the outfielder, the outfielder's arm strength, which arm the outfielder throws with, and so on—and make a decision to go or stay. Occasionally, when the coach hits a ground ball directly at an outfielder, on a prearranged signal the outfielder should bobble the ball as if mishandling it. As soon as the runner sees the ball bobbled, he should immediately break for second base.

The coach may put an infielder on second base to take throws for the outfielders. For safety reasons, do not allow sliding even on close plays.

Points can be awarded to players for smart decisions and aggressive running. Keep a chart of results. Players in each line could compete against each other.

Coaching Points

- Teach players that when they are stopping and returning to the base after rounding it to keep their eyes on the ball.
- Do not allow players to make too big a turn around the base and put themselves at risk of being tagged out.

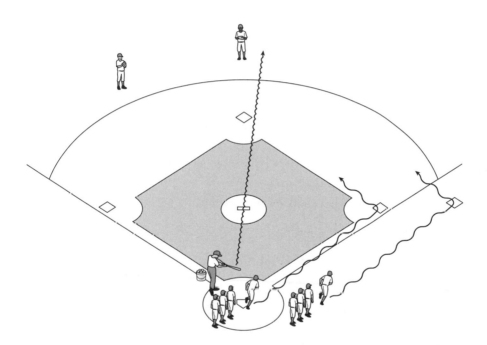

7.10 — Read and Run

Age: *12 and older*   **Skill Level:** ⚾⚾⚾⚾

Introduction

Joe Morgan once said that aggressive runners make the whole infield jumpy. That is what being aggressive is all about—keeping the defense on edge. This game teaches runners to read pitch trajectories and to advance any time the ball is thrown in the dirt. Runners work on getting good jumps. At the same time, catchers gain skill at blocking balls in the dirt, retrieving them, and making good throws to second in gamelike conditions.

Equipment

Bucket of baseballs, catcher's gear, bases, cones

Setup

- Two or more catchers are at the plate in full gear.
- Place a cone along the first-base line 5 feet (1.5 m) behind first base. (Additional cones may be used at the coach's discretion.)
- Runners with helmets form two lines—one at first base and one at the cone.
- One infielder is at second base.
- A coach stands 45 feet (15 m) from home plate with bucket of baseballs.

Procedure

A catcher assumes receiving position behind the plate. Runners in both lines take 15-foot (5 m) primary leads. Cones or other markers can be used to mark the spot where the runner's back foot should be. The coach acts as a feeder and throws a variety of pitches to the catcher. Anytime the ball hits the dirt, the runners must break for second base. The catcher blocks the ball and throws to second.

On balls that are not in the dirt, runners take a secondary lead and then return to the end of the opposite line from which they started. The next two runners take their places, and play resumes.

In this game the runners are playing against the catcher. If the catcher blocks the ball, award one point for the block. If the catcher's throw to second beats the runner from the line nearest to home plate, award two points. If the runner beats the throw, award the runner two points. To avoid injury, runners do not slide at second base. Alternate catchers every few throws.

Coaching Points

- Watch to make certain that catchers are not rushing their throws.
- Be sure that they are getting their feet under their hips before launching the ball.

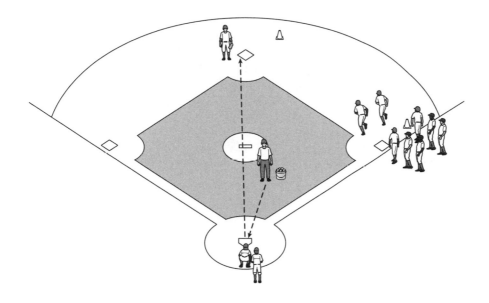

Take Three

Age: *12 and older*   **Skill Level:** 🔵🔵🔵🔵

Introduction

An old adage in baseball says that stealing third is easier than stealing second. Whether that is true or not, most teams don't spend enough time working to defend against the steal of third or to steal the base. This game creates multiple opportunities for players to work on this situation while using only part of the diamond. It is useful in training pitchers to hold runners close to second base with variations of their pickoff moves and deliveries. The game also helps catchers quicken their releases and work on reacting to steals or picking off runners at second. Runners receive training in leading off, reading pitchers, and getting a good break to third.

Equipment

Baseballs

Setup

- A batter is in the batter's box.
- A catcher in full gear is behind the plate.
- Pitchers form a line near the mound.
- A line of runners with helmets forms behind second base.
- Players are positioned at shortstop, second base, and third base.
- Optional: A coach is in the third-base coaching box.

Procedure

This game is similar to Cat and Mouse (page 174) except that the runners now start at second base. The first pitcher in line assumes stretch position on the rubber. He takes his sign and then can either pick at second base or throw a pitch. The first runner takes a primary lead at second base. If the pitcher throws home, the runner steals or takes a secondary lead on the pitch. If the runner goes, the catcher throws to third base on the steal. To avoid injuries, no sliding is allowed. If the throw beats the runner to the base, the runner is out. If the runner hesitates or slips, the catcher should try to pick the runner off second.

A runner must steal on one of the first three pitches during his time on the base. After each attempted steal, a new runner assumes a primary lead at second base. The batter is in the box only to create a gamelike atmosphere and should not swing at the pitches. The shortstop and second baseman should work on their skills at holding runners close to the base.

The defense gets two points for every successful stop; the running team gets one point for each steal. This game can be extremely competitive if the stakes are high enough. Give incentives for winning.

Coaching Points

- This game creates opportunities for coaches to train infielders, pitchers, and catchers on ways to hold runners close.
- Teach pitchers to vary their looks to second base and the timing of their pitches home.
- Watch to make sure that pitchers aren't falling into a pattern or telegraphing their throws with telltale body movements.

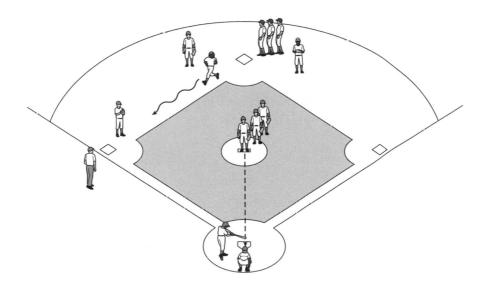

Long Pepper

Age: *12 and older*   **Skill Level:** ⚾⚾⚾⚾⚾

Introduction

This variation of the game of pepper can add some spice to a typical batting practice. First learned from Bob Bennett, the legendary skipper at Fresno State University, this game cranks up normal pepper a few notches and puts added pressure on batters to focus on their mechanics. The main objective of the game is to hit line drives and hard ground balls. The more ground balls the batter hits, the more reps he gets in batting practice. Instead of just trying to hit the ball, batters are given incentive to concentrate on the result of each swing, thereby focusing on contact and swing plane more often. The game gives more meaning to the phrase "live batting practice" and makes batting practice almost like a scrimmage. Players who work on keeping their swing compact and their swing plane downward are rewarded with more cuts.

Equipment

Bucket of baseballs, pitching machine, catcher's gear, L-screen

Setup

- Outfielders are stationed straightaway in left, center, and right.
- One catcher in full gear is behind home plate.
- Pitching machine set up in front of mound with coach attending.
- A batter is in the box.
- One batter is on deck; other players can be rotating through other hitting stations.

Procedure

Unless the batting-practice pitcher is skilled in throwing good pitches to hit, a pitching machine should be used here. The outfielders should be no more than 160 feet (60 m) from home plate. They are the targets for the hitters. How well batters hit determines how many swings they get in their live batting-practice session. To begin, each batter receives 25 points to use in his at-bat. After he uses up his 25 points, his at-bat ends and he rotates to the next station on the field.

Scoring can vary according to a coach's prerogative, but the main criteria should be to reward hard ground balls and line drives and penalize fly balls and popups. Give 1 point for each hard ground ball or line drive, fair or foul. A chopper or bounding ball is worth 3 points, and a popup or fly ball at the fielders is worth 10 points. Fly balls in the gaps could be given fewer points because they might result in extra-base hits. In theory, players can get 25 cuts in batting practice if they hit only line drives and hard ground balls.

Keeping a running tally from day to day adds a strong competitive element to everyday batting practice. Players hate to have their number of cuts limited in batting practice. This game puts the responsibility for their reps squarely on their shoulders.

Coaching Points

- Because the results of bad swings tend to be poor hits, coaches will find many opportunities to work with players' swing mechanics.
- Pay close attention to make sure that batters are taking their hands inside the ball on their swings.
- Give lots of positive reinforcement to players who hit line drives and hard ground balls.

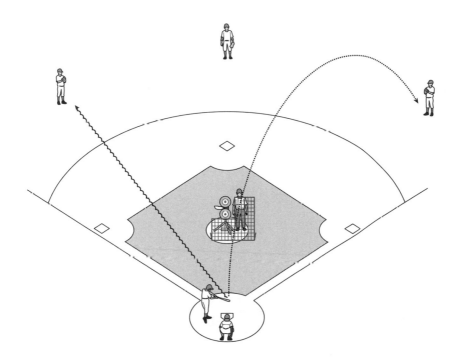

TEAM GAMES

8.1

Keystone Cops

Age: **All**   Skill Level: **All**

Introduction

In the early days of Hollywood, some of the zaniest movies made featured a band of misfit, clumsy, inept policemen called the Keystone Cops. They would run around in circles hitting each other and, rarely (if ever), catch the bad guys. This game gets its name from those Mack Sennett comedies because to the uninitiated it resembles a Keystone Cops movie. Besides being one of the most fun games that your players will engage in during the year, it teaches them patience, makes them hustle without their really knowing it, and creates camaraderie.

Equipment

Baseball, bases, bats, helmets, L-screen

Setup

- Divide the team into two squads, regardless of numbers.
- One team bats; the other fields.
- Use only two bases—home and second.
- With younger players, a coach should pitch.

Procedure

One team starts on offense and bats in order. One team plays defense. If a squad has fewer or more than nine players, allow players to decide where they will position themselves for maximum coverage. Because first base is not used in the game, no first baseman is needed, but one defensive player must be the catcher. Another important difference in this game is that the pitcher is part of the offensive team and is expected to pitch the ball where the hitter wants it pitched. He does not have to pitch from the regulation distance, but if he pitches from a shorter distance, an L-screen should be used, especially with younger players. The pitcher must not field any batted ball.

All outs in the game are force-outs. No sliding or tagging is allowed. No bunting is allowed. The catcher does not need gear, but he should stand well behind home plate to avoid being hit by foul tips.

When a player hits a ball, he must run diagonally across the diamond from home plate to second base. If the batter reaches second base before the defense fields the ball and throws it to a player covering second, the offensive team receives one point. If the ball is caught on the fly, the batter is out. One swinging strike or foul ball is an out. If a runner occupies second base and a succeeding batter hits a ground ball, the runner must run home. The defense then has the option of throwing home or throwing to second to make the out. If the ball is handled quickly enough, it is possible to make a double play. If the runner touches home, the offense receives another point. The exception would be if the batter is put out at second base for the third out before the runner scores. In that case the team does not gain a point. A player can also tag up at second base and try to score on a fly ball. After three outs, players change sides. As soon as all defensive players are off the field, the offensive pitcher may pitch to the batter.

After players have been playing the game for a while, they will figure out that if they are quick enough on and off the field, they can gain an advantage on the other team. They should not be told, but they should also come to the following conclusions: The catcher on defense should be the first batter for the team during the next half inning, the third baseman should be the first pitcher, and the outfielders should run immediately to the foul line after the third out so that they are off the field. Who says that practice can't be fun?

Coaching Point

○ The game creates numerous teachable moments, but the less the coach interrupts play, the more fun it is for the players.

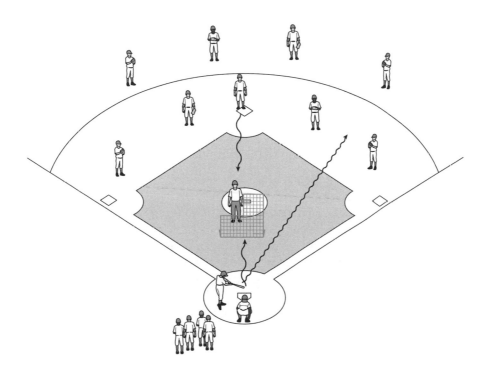

8.2 — Move Up

Age: *10 and older* **Skill Level:** *All*

Introduction

Why is it that even the least mobile player on the team, especially if he's left-handed, is always begging the coach for a chance to play shortstop? Well, this game, besides being gamelike, gives every player a chance to play shortstop, and every other position for that matter, while keeping the team hustling, focused, and having fun. Although the main objective of the game is to keep players loose, it also keeps batters focused on staying within themselves. Because making a mistake in this game keeps players from batting, they concentrate more on their fielding, throwing, and baserunning skills. The game also gives nonstarters a chance to show their value.

Equipment

Baseball, bases, bats, helmets, L-screen

Setup

- Place defensive players at all positions.
- Catchers rotate every few innings.
- Remaining players stay in the dugout and bat.
- The coach pitches.
- All fielding gloves are piled up to the foul side of first base.

Procedure

Coaches should put players at all the defensive positions except pitcher. For consistency, one of the coaches should pitch behind an L-screen, throwing pitches at batting-practice speed. The remaining players are given a batting order to follow.

Batters are allowed two swinging or called strikes. Coaches call the pitches. If a batter hits the ball and is safe at first base, he stays on the base and reacts to whatever the next batter does. Runners run on ground balls, tag on fly balls, and so on. When the third out in the inning is made, runners return to the dugout and bat again in their spot in the order. As long as they do not make out, they may remain in to bat. If an L-screen is used and a batted ball hits it, the coach determines whether it is a hit.

If the batter makes an out, he sprints to the glove pile, grabs his glove, and takes the place of the defender in right field. The right fielder moves up to center field, center goes to left, left moves to third, and so on. The first baseman throws his glove in the pile and runs in to take a spot in the batting rotation. After the rotation is complete, the next batter steps up and play resumes. After three outs, runners clear the bases before hitting resumes. If a runner is forced out at a base, he does not lose his batting turn. The batter who hit the ball grabs his glove and moves to right field. Batters cannot bunt, and base runners cannot steal.

If the coach deems that the runner made a bad judgment on the bases, the runner must get his glove and sprint to right field. Coaches should rotate catchers every few innings so that they have a chance to bat and field.

Scoring can be done in myriad ways: How long a player stays in to bat, who makes the fewest mistakes, and so on. Coaches should be creative and challenge their squads.

Coaching Points

- Freeze play when moments for positive reinforcement occur.
- Focus attention on mechanics and tactical thinking skills.

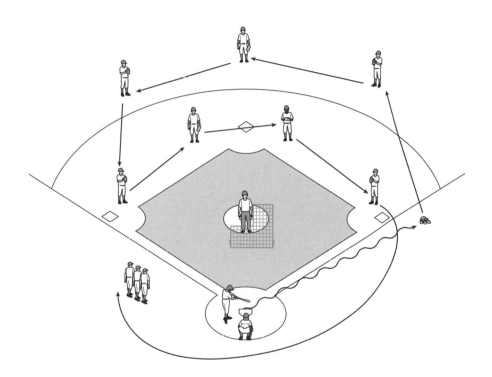

Situations

Age: *10 and older*   **Skill Level:** *All*

Introduction

Nothing teaches awareness and tactics better than games, but most players, unfortunately, do not play enough games to develop game sense. A solution to this problem would be to scrimmage every day, but that method is impractical for most teams because of the fragile nature of young pitching arms. The following game exposes players daily to situations that arise in games and presents many opportunities for coaches to instruct players in proper reaction to game situations. But these are only two of the goals of the game. Depending on a coach's individual philosophy, the game can also be used for conditioning, competition for positions, or motivation. In fact, this game is more valuable to a team than a scrimmage is. Scrimmages are random. Not all the situations that a coach may want to address will arise in a scrimmage because hitters don't always hit the ball where the coach might like them to. But because the coach controls the situations that occur in this game, that element of chance is eliminated.

Equipment

Two baseballs, bases, fungo bat, helmets, catcher's gear, cone

Setup

- Place one player at each defensive position, including pitcher.
- The remaining players, wearing helmets, line up in foul territory near home plate to serve as runners.
- The coach, with a fungo bat, stands near the batter's box.

Procedure

Defensive players assume ready positions. The pitcher throws a medium-speed fastball to the catcher. As the ball is crossing the plate, the coach hits a fungo. The first player in line runs as if he had just hit the ball. After each hit, the ball is returned to the pitcher and play continues in the same fashion. After three outs, clear the bases and begin a new inning. Defensive players remain on the field.

Be certain that runners don't run until the bat hits the ball. Use a cone to mark the starting point for runners.

Coaches can make substitutions at any time. Defensive players who are replaced become runners. When runners are on base, pitchers can try to pick them off, but stealing is not allowed. Sliding is permitted.

The coach controls the game. He can create any situation that he thinks his team needs to work on by hitting with the fungo accordingly. Virtually any situation that could occur in a real game can be reproduced in this game. If the coach wants to set up a bunt situation, he should square around as the pitch is being thrown and then roll the ball onto the field.

When either the runners or the defensive players make mistakes, the coach can explain and correct immediately, focusing attention on the errors and even using the freeze replay technique—having players replay the event in slow motion.

Normally, a nine-inning game can be played in less than a half hour. Because this game is mainly a defensive team game, give the defense one run per inning and see whether they can hold the offense to fewer runs. The object of the game is for the defense to win by not allowing more runs to be scored than they have been given. If the offense wins, the whole team should do some sort of conditioning exercise. This incentive usually helps players focus on reducing mistakes.

When the game is played daily, players get valuable repetition in recognizing offensive and defensive situations as they develop and react to them, improving their baseball sense dramatically.

Coaching Points

- Make certain that defenders make proper adjustments to the situation. Coaches should be stationed in the infield and outfield so that they can observe and correct.

- Make certain that all defenders move on every play.

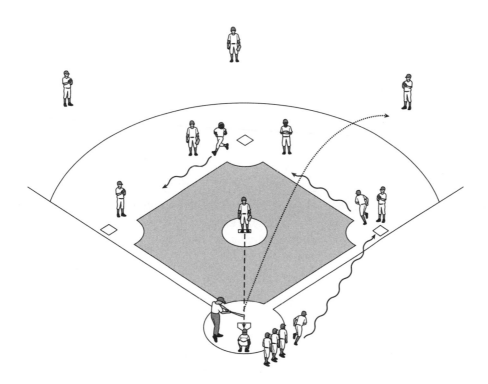

21 Outs

Age: *12 and older*   **Skill Level:** ●●●●

Introduction

Pitchers often get themselves in trouble by trying to be too fine with their pitches. Instead of just letting the batter hit the ball to one of the seven fielders behind them, pitchers sometimes feel as if they have to make every out by themselves. Being too fine with pitches often leads to walks, and walks more often than not lead to big innings. Much truth is contained in the phrase "Walks will kill ya." This game, which I learned from high school coaching legend Dick Birmingham of Springfield, Missouri, forces pitchers to let batters hit the ball. Its objective is to let the defense handle the ball and make outs. It also should convince the pitching staff that throwing fastballs for strikes means that the ball will be hit at someone most of the time. The game, by its nature, allows teams to work on their defense, helping them create a sense of pride in their work. It gives pitchers practice in game situations while not overworking them before their next start. At the same time, it gives nonstarters a chance to hit against the first team and prove their value.

Equipment

Baseballs, bases, stopwatch

Setup

- ◎ Defensive players take places at all positions.
- ◎ Players not on defense bat.
- ◎ Coaches take a good viewing position on the field from which they will be able to focus play.

Procedure

The game is basically regulation baseball with a notable exception—the defense remains on the field for seven innings. The nonstarters bat in order each inning. Coaches may substitute pitchers, but teams do not switch sides after each half inning. Several other rules differentiate this game from a regular game:

1. No walks
2. No strikeouts
3. No curveballs
4. No bunting
5. No stealing
6. No sliding

After three outs are made, the bases are cleared and the offense bats again. When the defense makes 21 outs the game is over.

Use a stopwatch when playing this game. Start the watch with the first pitch and don't stop it until 21 outs have been made. The game should take no longer than 30 to 40 minutes to play. Teams can be motivated to beat their best time each time they play it. Post the time prominently in the dugout or in the locker room to give players a daily reminder.

The reasoning behind the rules is simple. They force pitchers to throw strikes and not be too fine with their pitches. Taking away stealing and bunting helps the pitchers focus. All they have to do is think about the batter. Eliminating sliding lessens the chance of injury in what is essentially an intrasquad scrimmage.

Have all pitchers warmed up and ready on the sidelines before they go into the game to pitch. Pitchers should only throw one or two innings. Nonstarting pitchers chart pitches. A good game should require 50 to 75 pitches.

Coaching Points

- Make certain that players treat the game seriously. After playing the game a few times, players will begin to see the value of just playing the game and not worrying about the score.
- Use teachable moments to freeze play and explain or positively reinforce good play.

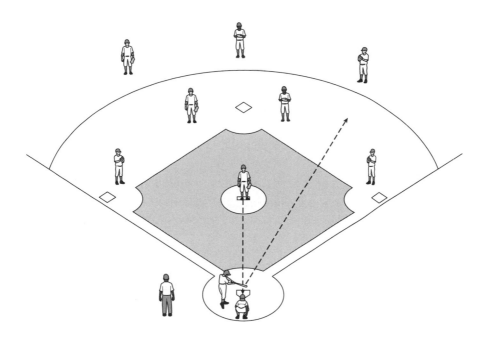

8.5 — Bingo, Bango, Bongo

Age: *12 and older*   **Skill Level:** ⚾⚾⚾⚾

Introduction

A great concern of most coaches is trying to keep the whole team involved during batting practice. By its nature, batting practice lends itself to down time. Players congregate in the outfield, lackadaisically chase ground balls and fly balls, and sometimes view the time as an opportunity to relax. Coaches over the years have gotten extremely creative in making sure that all players are involved during batting practice. This game is an alternative that not only keeps all players busy but also adds a gamelike element to batting practice. It forces players to concentrate on more than just ball striking and requires shaggers in the field to react to batted balls as they were playing a real game. By spelling out what the hitter must do before taking his batting-practice cuts, it puts pressure on him to perform. In addition, the game improves a base runner's ability to react to developing situations in games. (Author's note: The title comes from an old song by the Andrews Sisters. I'm not sure why I call it this. Maybe it's a subconscious association with the golf game of the same name.)

Equipment

Bucket of baseballs, pitching L-screen, rubber throw-down base or cone, helmets

Setup

- Set up batting practice in normal fashion.
- Place a cone or throw-down base along the first-base foul line 180 feet (55 m) from home plate.
- Give a batting-order number to all players.
- The player with the last number starts at first base.

Procedure

Set up batting practice as normal using as many stations as deemed necessary. Begin batting practice with the last batter in the day's order stationed at first base wearing a helmet. Place an additional base or cone 180 feet (55 m) from home plate along the right-field foul line. The game progresses as follows: (1) The first pitch to the batter is treated as a hit-and-run situation. The runner takes off for second on the pitch and looks in after three steps to see where the ball is. If the ball is hit in the air, the runner retreats to first base and the batter tries again on the next pitch. If the hit-and-run is executed successfully, the runner stops at second base. (2) The second pitch to the batter is treated as a sacrifice bunt. The batter attempts to sacrifice the runner to third base. (3) The third pitch to the batter is treated as a suicide squeeze. On this pitch the batter must get the ball on the ground no matter where it is thrown. The runner takes off for home, reacting to the pitcher (stretch or windup), and runs 75 feet (23 m) down the line before peeling off. If the batter completes all three stages—bingo, bango, bongo—he gets the remainder of his swings allocated for batting practice that day. On the last pitch of his turn, the batter must drag bunt and sprint to first base. He then becomes the runner for the next hitter, and Bingo, Bango, Bongo starts over.

To create incentive for batters to execute, use this alternative version: If the batter pops up the hit-and-run pitch, he must immediately drop his bat and sprint to the base or cone located 180 feet (55 m) down the line. He then takes a place on the field, and becomes the last batter in the batting-practice order. Use the same disincentive if the batter pops up a bunt.

Coaching Points

- Use the game to reinforce baserunning, fielding, and throwing skills.
- Challenge players to perform under pressure. If they fail at any one of the situations, make them go into the field and lose their turn at bat until later.

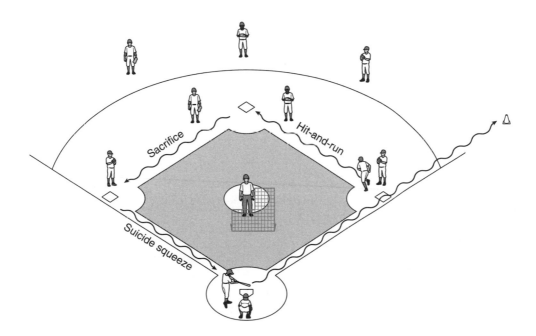

Bunt Game

Age: *12 and older*   **Skill Level:** ⚾⚾⚾⚾

Introduction

This game develops the infield skills needed to react successfully to game situations that involve bunting—drag bunts, sacrifices, squeeze bunts, push bunts, fake bunt and hit, and so on—and it will develop each of these various bunting skills necessary to executing the offensive bunt game. To be effective, it should be played at least once per week. The game involves the entire team split into two separate squads of equal number if possible. The squads should remain the same each time the game is played. This approach leads to a season-long competition that increases team camaraderie. The game should take no more than 30 minutes of practice time if players hustle between innings.

Equipment

Several baseballs, bats, bases, catcher's gear, cones

Setup

- Divide the team into two equal squads.
- The defensive team occupies all infield positions—first base, second base, short-stop, third base, and catcher. Extra players remain in foul territory until they rotate into the game. No outfielders are needed.
- To provide consistency of pitches, the coach should pitch or a pitching machine should be used.
- The offensive team determines its batting order. Each player has a turn at bat even if he is not playing in the field in a particular inning.

Procedure

One team is in the field, and the other is at bat. Teams take turns batting. After three outs they switch sides.

Rules for the team at bat: The first batter must drag bunt. If he is out at first base, the next batter must drag bunt until a runner is safe at first. After a runner is on first, the next batter must sacrifice bunt. If the runner on first is forced out at second base, the next batter must also sacrifice until there are three outs or the runner is successfully sacrificed to second base. Once a runner successfully reaches second base with less than three outs, the next batter has the option of either drag bunting, push bunting, or using the fake-bunt-and-slash technique. When a runner reaches third base safely with less than three outs, the next batter must perform a suicide squeeze bunt on the next pitch, no matter where it is.

Rules for the team in the field: Pitchers must only throw fastballs. There are no walks, called strikeouts, or hit batsmen. Batters bat until they successfully bunt the ball or foul off strike three. If runners are on the bases, pitchers may attempt pickoff plays. Important: Infielders must stay on the infield dirt until the ball reaches home plate before they charge to cover the bunt. Infielders must assume normal positions before each pitch.

Suggested scoring: The team at bat receives one point for each successful bunt. For example, if the first drag bunter reaches first, the team receives a point. If the next batter successfully sacrifices the runner to second base, the team receives another point, etc. On the squeeze play, the runner should not slide. Catchers should not block the plate but instead treat the play as a force situation. If the runner beats the ball to the plate, score a point for the offense. If the ball beats the runner, the runner is out. If the bunt is fielded and there is no play on the runner, but the defense puts the batter out at first base for the third out, the inning is over, but the offensive team receives a point for the successful squeeze bunt. Scoring continues the same way for each stage of the game. Coaches can decide to add plus or minus points as they see fit.

Length of game: The game should be played for three or four innings—whatever can be accomplished in a half hour.

Coaching Points

- Coaches can freeze play often to reinforce teachable moments. Compliment smart judgment and freely point out mistakes.
- Watch that players use proper bunting technique.
- Make sure that defenders do not charge too early. Doing so would give them an unfair advantage.

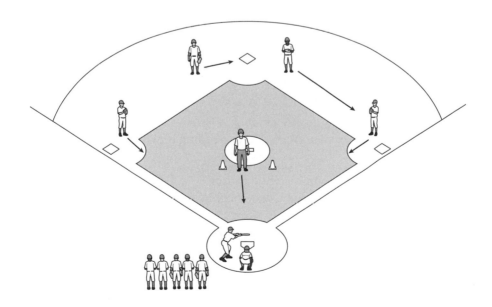

8.7 ── Combat Scrimmage ──

Age: *12 and older*   **Skill Level:** ●●●●

Introduction

Pressure! Every coach tries to prepare his team to stay calm under pressure and just play the game. There is no magic pill that players can take to keep them cool and poised at game time, but if they are comfortable reacting to pressure situations in practice, they will probably confront them more effectively in games. Instead of a normal scrimmage, this variation puts pressure on the defense, and offense, every inning. Each inning, situations are created that give an offense a chance to capitalize and a defense a chance to extinguish a fire. Facing situations such as these in practice makes players more accustomed to them in real games and less likely to make mistakes or fold under pressure. Coaches can use this game to test players' toughness in combat conditions or put them in situations in which they have failed in the past to retest them. Each inning features a common game situation.

Equipment

Baseballs, bats, gloves

Setup

- Divide the team in half.
- One side plays the other as in a normal scrimmage with variations.
- If not enough players are available to field two teams, place one team on defense and let the other players bat. After three outs, players clear the bases and bat again with the same team on defense but under different circumstances.
- Change sides every half inning.
- The coach can interrupt play at any time.

Procedure

Each inning begins with a pressure situation. The following list is merely a guide. Coaches can develop their own progression according to what they think their team needs to work on.

- First inning: Begin the inning with a runner on first and no outs. Play out the inning. Switch sides after three outs. Begin the bottom half of the inning with the same situation.
- Second inning: Runner on second, no outs.
- Third inning: Runners on first and third, one out.
- Fourth inning: Nobody on, no outs.
- Fifth inning: Runner on third, one out.

- Sixth inning: Bases loaded, one out.
- Seventh inning: Runners on first and second, one out.
- Eighth inning: Runners on second and third, two outs.
- Ninth inning: Nobody on base, one out.

Coaches can switch fielders and hitters at will, and they can put in pitchers who have had problems working in tight situations in the past.

Score the game normally. Keep the same teams throughout the season if possible. Keep standings if the game is played regularly. Coaches can even use this setup when scrimmaging other teams. Most would find it much more valuable than a normal scrimmage.

Coaching Point

- Stop the scrimmage whenever necessary to point out positive aspects of play or errors in judgment.

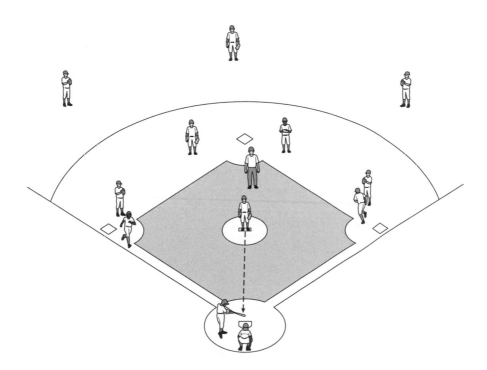

8.8 — Hit-and-Run

Age: *12 and older*   **Skill Level:** ●●●●

Introduction

When executed properly, the hit-and-run play can energize an offense and let the air out of a defense. Although the main goal of the hit-and-run play is to help a team avoid the double play, a secondary goal, especially for an aggressive offense, is to advance runners to third or home, depending on where they've started. An additional advantage of the play is that it puts the defense on edge. This game, a variation of Right Side (page 154), engages not only the hitters but also the base runners, and it creates numerous opportunities for teams to hone their hit-and-run proficiency.

Equipment

L-screen, cones, baseballs, bats, pitching machine (optional)

Setup

- Divide the team in half.
- One team bats; the other is on defense.
- The offense bats in order.
- One offensive player starts on first base.
- Place a cone in the base line about 15 feet (5 m) on the third-base side of second base.
- Place another cone in center field in a direct line from home plate through the cone in the infield.
- The defense assumes positions on the right-field side of the cones. No players are in left field, at shortstop, or at third base.
- A catcher is optional; a sock net can be used in place of a catcher.

Procedure

The defense assumes positions on the field. One player from the offensive team takes a primary lead at first base. Another offensive player is at bat. Every pitch is considered a hit-and-run. Coaches should pitch to keep the game fair.

When the coach throws the first ball, the runner at first breaks for second. If the batter misses the pitch or pops it up, the runner returns to first. If the batter hits the pitch on the ground or on a line to the outfield, the runner continues sprinting to third. If the ball is hit on the ground and fielded in the infield, the fielders have the opportunity to attempt the double play or to make an out at first or second base. After hitting the ball, the batter must run to first base. He becomes the next runner, and play continues.

For this game, two called or swinging strikes is an out. Any ball hit to the left field side of the cones, fouls included, counts as two outs. Six outs are allowed per inning. After six outs, teams switch sides. Three or four innings can be played in about 15 minutes.

Because the hit-and-run has several objectives, scoring should reflect those goals. Score one point for every runner who reaches second safely and two points for a runner who gets beyond second. Because there is no third baseman, outfielders will not throw to third; the assumption is that the runner made it there safely.

Coaches need to watch closely so that runners at first do not take too big a primary lead or leave too early. Doing this would give the offense an unfair advantage.

Coaching Points

- Watch that runners do not look in toward the plate until they have taken a few strides toward second. Watching the ball prevents runners from getting a good jump.
- Teach runners to sprint on the hit-and-run. If the batter hits a line drive in a game that an infielder catches, he would be unable to get back to the base anyway.

Relay, Relay, Relay

Age: *12 and older*   **Skill Level:** ●●●●

Introduction

When an outfielder or infielder overthrows a relay man, a runner can advance farther, and perhaps even score. This game creates real-time situations that force outfielders and infielders to become quicker and more accurate with their throws. It also gives runners a chance to work on their ability to run bases economically by making short turns. Players will become more proficient at working on double cuts and relays and be able to recognize opportunities to stop runners from taking extra bases.

Equipment

Balls, buckets, catcher's gear

Setup

- Place buckets in the outfield gaps in right-center field and left-center field near the fence or wall.
- Have fielders at all positions.
- Other players form two lines of runners—one midway between first base and second base and the other midway between home and first.

Procedure

The game begins with a runner in position midway between first base and second base and another between home and first. All fielders are in ready position at their spots on the field. A coach or extra player places a ball into an empty bucket in the gap between left and center or between right and center. As soon as the ball is put into the bucket, the outfielders near the bucket sprint to the ball as if it were an extra-base hit in the gap. One runner in each line begins running at the same time. Outfielders retrieve the ball and make the appropriate throw called for. All players rotate into positions to either cover a base, back up a base, or serve as a relay.

Score one point for each run or extra base the runners get. Score three points for every time the defense cuts down a runner at the plate or at third base. No sliding is allowed. If the ball beats the runner score points for the defense; if the runner beats the ball to the base score a point for the offense. Runners should be aggressive and force the defense into making quick decisions about whether to let a ball through or cut it and throw to another base. Defenses should execute double relays to either third or home. Coaches should rotate players frequently from defense to offense. Give incentives to the defense for winning the contest.

Coaching Points

● Review field coverage on extra-base hits for each position.

● Teach players to give clear oral and visual signals on relays.

● Make sure that players know to change their body alignment when the ball is in the air so that when they receive a throw, they are in position to make the next throw.

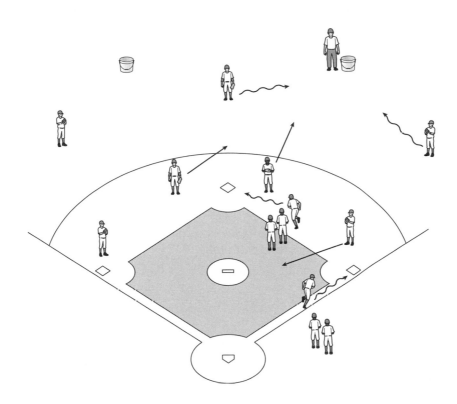

Double-Steal Challenge

8.10

Age: *12 and older*   **Skill Level:** ⚾⚾⚾⚾⚾

Introduction

Especially in high school baseball, the importance of the first-and-third double steal cannot be overestimated. Many a game has been lost because teams did not know how to handle the pressure of the potential double steal. Therefore, teams need to be able to run the play on offense successfully as well as be able to defend against its use. This game enables teams to develop the strategies and tactics needed to execute and defend against the double steal.

Equipment

Baseballs, bases, gloves, helmets

Setup

- Infielders, including a pitcher and catcher, assume their positions.
- The remaining players, including backup infielders, gather into two equally divided groups at first base and third base.
- One player from each group, wearing a helmet, takes a position on each of those bases.
- The coach observes from a position in the middle of the infield.

Procedure

The pitcher assumes his position on the rubber and gets his sign from the catcher. The runners on the bases take their primary leads, and the game begins. Using techniques that the team has learned, the runners attempt to execute the double steal and challenge the defense to get them out. They may execute the early break, the delayed steal, the straight steal, and so forth. The defense reacts to the double steal using all defensive tactics in the team's arsenal.

Before starting the game both the defense and the offense must agree on a new set of signs to use that the other side doesn't know. This aids in creating gamelike conditions and real-time pressure. The coach can tell the offense and defense what play to run, and they can then signal each other with their personalized signs.

Keep the scoring of the game simple to keep players focused on the objectives. For example, the defense wins if it records 5 outs before the offense steals 10 bases. Coaches can alter the scoring method in many ways to enhance the game. Substitute freely on defense so that all team members have a chance to make tactical decisions.

Coaching Points

- Make certain that defensive players react on each play. Defenders have a tendency to become lax if they know that they won't be involved in a play.
- Teach all players to fake cuts and run hard to their areas of responsibility. This activity helps sell a play and prevents runners from getting good jumps.

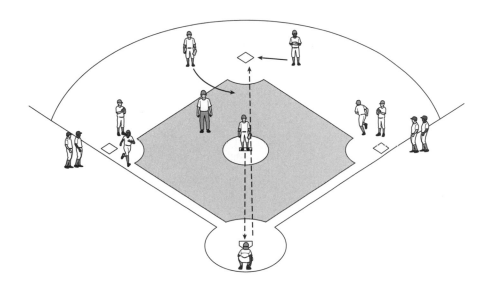

PRACTICE PLANNING

Practice Plan 1

5 Minutes Dynamic Warm-Up

Running backward, carioca, high-knee skips, sprints, butt kicks, and so on.

5 Minutes Dynamic Stretching

Run-in-place arm circles, walking lunges, side-lunge squats, lateral high-knee steps, ankle circles, RDLs (Romanian deadlifts); vary daily.

10 Minutes Throwing Warm-Up

- Whoosh (page 10) (especially in initial practices)
- One-Knee Throwing (page 8)
- Hit the Target Squarely (page 4)
- Progressive Long Toss (page 16)

10 Minutes Throwing

- Touch 'Em All (page 12)
- Four Corners Against the Clock (page 18)

Practice Plan 2

5 Minutes Dynamic Warm-Up

Running backward, carioca, high-knee skips, sprints, butt kicks, and so on.

5 Minutes Dynamic Stretching

Run-in-place arm circles, walking lunges, side-lunge squats, lateral high-knee steps, ankle circles, RDLs; vary daily.

10 Minutes Throwing Warm-Up

- Yoga Toss (page 6)
- One-Knee Throwing (page 8)
- Hit the Target Squarely (page 4)
- Progressive Long Toss (page 16)

10 Minutes Fielding

- Goalie (page 48)
- Crossover (page 34)
- Mass Fungo (page 56)

Practice Plan 3

5 Minutes Dynamic Warm-Up

Running backward, carioca, high-knee skips, sprints, butt kicks, and so on.

5 Minutes Dynamic Stretching

Run-in-place arm circles, walking lunges, side-lunge squats, lateral high-knee steps, ankle circles, RDLs; vary daily.

10 Minutes Throwing Warm-Up

- One-Knee Throwing (page 8)
- Hit the Target Squarely (page 4)
- Progressive Long Toss (page 16)

10 Minutes Pitching

- In the Box (page 92)
- Dueling Pitchers (U-R-O-U-T) (page 102)

Practice Plan 4

5 Minutes Dynamic Warm-Up

Running backward, carioca, high-knee skips, sprints, butt kicks, and so on.

5 Minutes Dynamic Stretching

Run-in-place arm circles, walking lunges, side-lunge squats, lateral high-knee steps, ankle circles, RDLs; vary daily.

20 Minutes Throwing Warm-Up

- Progressive Long Toss (page 16)
- Four Corners (page 2)
- Other throwing games; vary daily

10 Minutes Position-Specific Drills

Players should work rapidly through skill sets.

- Infielders work in pairs on fielding skills—forehands, backhands, slow rollers, and so on.
- Outfielders work with the coach on ground balls, do-or-die plays, fly balls, communications, and so on.
- Catchers work on framing, blocking, and throwing.

20 Minutes Hitting Stations

Divide players into equal groups and have them rotate quickly from station to station.

- Flip It (page 138)
- Short Toss (page 152)
- Target Hitting (page 134)
- Triangle Hitting (page 158)

Practice Plan 5

5 Minutes Dynamic Warm-Up

Vary daily with short-burst running drills; use plyometric ladders, cones, and hurdles to add variety.

5 Minutes Dynamic Stretching

Run-in-place arm circles, walking lunges, side-lunge squats, lateral high-knee steps, ankle circles, RDLs; vary daily.

20 Minutes Throwing Warm-Up

- Progressive Long Toss (page 16)
- Stars (page 22)
- Other throwing games; vary daily

5 Minutes Position-Specific Drills

Players should work rapidly through skill sets.

- Infielders work in pairs on fielding skills—choose specific skills to work on for the day.
- Outfielders work on playing the fence, going back on balls, and fielding line drives.
- Catchers work on framing, fielding bunts, and throwing to first and third.

10 Minutes Baserunning

- Running to first base
- Bobble and Go! (page 184)
- Advancing From Second (page 172)

15 Minutes Hitting Stations

Divide players into equal groups and have them rotate quickly from station to station.

- Soft toss
- Target Hitting (page 134)
- Live batting practice
- Walk-Through (page 160)

Practice Plan 6

5 Minutes Dynamic Warm-Up

Vary daily with short-burst running drills; use plyometric ladders, cones, and hurdles to add variety.

5 Minutes Dynamic Stretching

Run-in-place arm circles, walking lunges, side-lunge squats, lateral high-knee steps, ankle circles, RDLs; vary daily.

20 Minutes Throwing Warm-Up

- Four Corners Against the Clock (page 18)
- Long toss (use as last game in warm-up session)
- Other throwing games; vary daily

5 Minutes Position-Specific Drills

Players should work rapidly through skill sets.

- Middle infielders work on pivots and feeds at second base, balls in the hole.
- Corner infielders work on blocking balls, backhand plays, and fielding bunts.
- Outfielders work on ground balls, turning and running to spots, and communication on balls in the gaps.
- Catchers work on blocking the plate, throwing to second, wild pitches, and fielding foul balls.

25 Minutes Team Scrimmage

15 Outs (shortened variation of 21 Outs [page 200])—time game and record results

Practice Plan 7

5 Minutes Dynamic Warm-Up

Use ladders, cones for shuttle drills, hurdles, and so on; vary running daily.

5 Minutes Dynamic Stretching

Run-in-place arm circles, leg swings, Spiderman lunges, side-lunge squats, ankle circles, RDLs; vary daily.

15 Minutes Throwing Warm-Up

- Partner throwing—one knee, stride drill, step-behind with arm swing, and so on.
- Four Corners Against the Clock (page 18)
- Long toss

20 Minutes Position-Specific Games

Players should work rapidly through skill sets.

- Middle infielders: Soft Hands (page 24), Get There! (page 44), Double-Play Rotation (page 36)
- Corner infielders: Hot-Corner Reaction (page 52), Z Ball Reaction (page 64), Slow-Roller Throwing (page 60)
- Pitchers, in bullpen with catchers: Location, Location, Location (page 94)
- Catchers, in pairs (when not in bullpen): Sway and Frame (page 118), Catcher Challenge (page 112)
- Outfielders: Five Alive (page 70), Hustle! (page 74), Line Drive (page 80), Do or Die (page 76)

20 Minutes Hitting Stations

Divide players into equal groups and have them rotate quickly from station to station.

- Flip It (page 138)
- Read the Pitch (page 150)
- Triangle Hitting (page 158)
- Right Side (page 154)

20 Minutes Team Hitting

- Hit-and-Run (page 208)
- Use freeze replays

5 Minutes Cool-Down

Divide players equally at the bases. On command, they sprint home to first, delay steal at first, straight steal at second, tag up and score from third. Each player makes two rotations.

Practice Plan 8

5 Minutes Dynamic Warm-Up

Use ladders, cones for shuttle drills, hurdles, and so on; vary running daily.

5 Minutes Dynamic Stretching

Run-in-place arm circles, leg swings, Spiderman lunges, side-lunge squats, ankle circles, RDLs; vary daily.

15 Minutes Throwing Warm-Up

- Partner throwing—one knee, stride drill, step-behind with arm swing, and so on.
- Globetrotter (page 20)
- Long toss

25 Minutes Hitting

Bingo, Bango, Bongo (page 202)—divide team into four rotating groups: one hitting, one baserunning, and two in the field; players waiting to bat are tee hitting into sock net

10 Minutes Team Defense and Baserunning

Double-Steal Challenge (page 212)—substitute players frequently

25 Minutes Team Game

Combat Scrimmage (page 206)—set up situations, use different pitchers every inning, and substitute freely

5 Minutes Cool-Down

Divide players equally at the bases. On command, they sprint home to first, delay steal at first, straight steal at second, tag up and score from third. Each player makes two rotations.

Practice Plan 9

5 Minutes Dynamic Warm-Up

Vary daily with short-burst running drills; use plyometric ladders, cones, and hurdles to add variety.

5 Minutes Dynamic Stretching

Run-in-place arm circles, leg swings, Spiderman lunges, side-lunge squats, ankle circles, RDLs; vary daily.

15 Minutes Position-Specific Drills and Games

Choose from the variety of drills and games listed previously.

25 Minutes Team Defense

Situations (page 198)—place players at all defensive positions and use extras as base runners. Try to create as many situations as possible; substitute defenders frequently.

20 Minutes Hitting Stations

Divide players into equal groups and have them rotate quickly from station to station.

- Long Tee (page 180)
- Soft toss
- Flip It (page 138)
- Triangle Hitting (page 158)

20 Minutes Team Game

Move Up (page 196)—use a coach as pitcher. Keep stats on fielding (putouts, assists, errors) and discuss results afterward.

Tom O'Connell has over 30 years of amateur and professional baseball coaching experience. A Major League Baseball recommending scout since 1986, O'Connell has worked for the Cincinnati Reds, the Los Angeles Dodgers, and the 2008 World Series champion Philadelphia Phillies. A recipient of numerous state and national awards for his coaching, O'Connell was named the 1991 Wisconsin Baseball Man of the Year, elected president of the American Baseball Coaches Association (ABCA) in 2002, named the 2004 ABCA Coach of the Year, and inducted into the ABCA Hall of Fame in 2007.

O'Connell is a contributing writer for the *Collegiate Baseball Newsletter* and author of numerous articles in baseball publications such as *Touching All Bases* and the *ABCA Quarterly Digest*. He also wrote *Coaching Youth Baseball* and *Coaching Baseball Technical and Tactical Skills* for the American Sport Education Program.

O'Connell lives in Milwaukee, Wisconsin.